THE
BOOK
OF
FAITH

Franklin Hunt, Th.D., D.D.

FOREWORD

This book is not intended to be a complete study of the subject on faith. Hundreds of books have been written on faith and I am sure that hundreds more will be. The purpose of this book is to put the subject in simple language so that the average reader can understand what faith is, how it works and how to use it. Each chapter is a complete sermon, within itself. Each of these sermons have been preached numerous times all across the USA and in several other nations.

During eight years of evangelistic preaching, in revivals, conferences, camp meetings and conventions, I received more than ten thousand testimonies of miracle healings. Every kind of healing and deliverance that I can imagine was included in these testimonies. Now, after thirty four years of pastoring, thousands more testimonies have come in!

These messages have gone out on tape, CD, radio and television. Every day, I get testimonies of other healings and miracles! Now, at last, the sermons are in print, in this Book Of Faith! I sincerely believe that many people will be healed and delivered while reading this book. If you are one of those, I encourage you to write to me. I would love to hear from you.

My purpose is to get the Word out. My prayer is that every reader will be blessed.

Franklin Hunt
P.O. Box 62
Fayetteville, N. C. 28302

CHAPTER 1

WHAT IS FAITH?

The majority of my preaching has been on Faith! I have preached and taught so much on faith that, people who know me, call me the "Faith Preacher". I have been asked many times why I preach so much on Faith. I reply, "Because it does not matter what else you preach on, you can not have it without faith".

This statement is true! You can preach on Salvation, but you can not be saved without faith! The Bible says by Grace you are saved through faith! You can preach on prayer, but your prayers will not be answered without faith! The Bible says when you pray, believe that you receive and you shall have! You can preach on living right, but you can not live right without faith! The Bible says, without faith it is impossible to please God! So we are saved by faith, we live by faith, we walk by faith, we are justified by faith, we please God by faith, our prayers are answered by faith, faith is counted to us for Righteousness and we will die by faith or go in the Rapture by faith! So it behooves us to know what faith is!

So what is Faith?

In this chapter, I am going to tell you what faith is, but in doing so, I am going to tell you what faith is not! I may uproot someone's theology, but I promise you I will set you back out in good Scriptural ground. (We all need to be uprooted sometimes. I do not mind being uprooted, if you will set me back out in the Word!)

FAITH IS NOT SEEING

The first thing I want you to know, is that Faith is not seeing!

If the Bible contrasts any two things, it contrasts faith and sight! The Bible says, "We walk by faith and not by sight". Say that to yourself! Get it in your spirit! We walk by faith and not by sight!

The world says, "Seeing is believing", but the Bible requires us to believe what we have no visible evidence of, whatsoever! We have to believe what we have not seen! Faith is the substance of things hoped for, the evidence of things not seen! I do not need faith to believe that this is a book, or that I have on clothes! I can see those things! It takes faith to believe what you have not seen and can not see! So according to the Bible, believing is seeing!

When I was in College, a Professor challenged me on this. He said, "I do not believe anything I cannot see." I asked him, "Do you believe you have a brain?" He said "Yes" I said, "Have you ever seen it?" You see, he had great faith, for I did not believe he had any brains. Only a fool will say he does not believe anything he can not see! I do not see how a black cow eats green grass and gives white milk, which makes yellow butter, but I am not going to eat dry toast until I figure it out! I will let the cow worry about it! I do not see how water running over a wheel, generates electricity, that makes the lights burn, but I am not going to sit in the dark, because I do not understand it!

That is how it is with God's Word! I do not understand how Jesus bore my sins and sicknesses and sorrows, but I am not going to stay in sin and sickness and sorrow, because I do not understand it! I am going to be saved, healed and joyful! I am going to take it by faith!

If I did not believe what I could not see, I would never cut another watermelon! I have cut some green ones and some rotten ones, but I still believe there are some good watermelons out there! If I did not believe what I could not see, I would never listen to the radio or watch the television! Later in this book, I will talk more about these things, but for now, I just want you to know that faith is not seeing! God requires us to believe what we can not see!

The Professor who argued with me said that every time Jesus did a miracle, he did it instantaneously, but this is not true. Jesus did many instantaneous miracles, but He also did many miracles that required people to act to on their faith!

For example, when he healed the ten lepers, it was not instantaneous. Now he could instantly heal leprosy, for when he came down for the Mount of transfiguration, he met a leper who said, "Lord, if you are willing, you can make me whole." Jesus said, "I am willing." He touched the man and instantly his leprosy was healed! (Matt. 8:1-3) But to the ten lepers, he did not pray for them or touch them. Instead, he said, "Go show yourselves to the Priest." Now the Old Testament had said if a man has leprosy and his leprosy goes away, then he should show himself to the priest. The Priest would keep him in a room for seven days and then look at him again. If his leprosy was still gone, he was allowed to go free! (Lev. 13 and 14) But Jesus told these men to go to the Priest, while the leprosy was all over them! So they started to the Priest! If they had been like some of us, they would have said, "I feel like a fool going to the Priest with this leprosy all over me."

But they had faith! They started toward the Temple with the leprosy all over them and the Bible says, "AS THEY WENT THEY WERE CLEANSED"! (Lu. 17:12-14) While they were walking along, one said "Hey, mine is going away!" Then another one said, "Mine is going away!" and by the time they reached the temple, all ten were cleansed, because they acted on faith!

A Blind man came to Jesus and he did not get instantly healed! Now Jesus could instantly heal blindness, because when He passed by Bartimaeus, the man cried out, "Jesus, thou Son of David, have mercy on me." The crowd tried to quiet him but he cried louder! When Jesus stopped and asked him what he wanted, he answered that he wanted to see. Jesus touched him and instantly he was healed! (Mk. 10:46-52) But now there comes another blind man to him and Jesus did not instantly heal him! You see this man left in worse condition than he came! Have you ever been prayed for and hurt worse afterward than you did before? I have! That is not the time to be discouraged, that is the time to rejoice, because the Devil is trying to talk you out of your healing! If Satan is causing you to hurt worse, it must be because he knows you are about to receive a Miracle!

So Jesus did not instantly heal this man! Instead, He spat on the ground and made mud plasters and put them over the man's eyes and then told him to go wash in a pool! You see, the man left in worse condition, because he came blind and left blind and blindfolded! Can you see the skeptics saying, "Who would send a blind man to wash in a pool? You need to use common sense. He could fall in and drown!" Sometimes the words, "common sense" are an excuse for unbelief! Many times in the Bible, God required people to do things that did not make sense to man! So often, when God tells us to do something, we let so called "common sense" get in the way of our faith! This man did not rely on "common sense", he walked by faith! I believe he had this kind of faith: "If someone will show me the way to the pool, I will find my own way back!" So he went and washed and came seeing! (Jn. 9:7-15) He walked by faith and not by sight! I could go on and on and show you many examples where God did not always do instant miracles, but instead, required people to act on Faith!

Jesus taught this lesson with a fig tree, that He cursed! I have heard many people teach on the fig tree and they all teach it wrong! They teach that Jesus cursed the fig tree, because it did not have any fruit and if you don't hurry up and get some fruit, He is going to curse you! (That teaching will really make you shout, won't it?) The fact is, Jesus did not curse the tree because it did not have fruit! Your Bible says, "It was not the season for figs." Now how could the tree have figs if it was not the season for figs? Then why did Jesus curse the tree? He cursed it to teach His disciples a lesson in faith!

Notice what actually happened. They were on their way into the city. Here stood this fig tree, big, leafy and bushy. Jesus simply spoke to it and said, "No man will eat fruit of you from henceforth." That is all He did! He did not join hands with the Disciples and gather around it and scream at it and demand that it die! He simply spoke to it and walked away. Now what happened? Did the tree crumble and fall to the ground? No! It just stood there, just as green and leafy and bushy as it was before Jesus spoke to it! So they went into the city then out of the city and then the next day they are on their way to the city again! Peter looked at the tree and it had begun to wither.

Peter said to the Lord that the fig tree He had cursed the day before was now withering. Now here is the lesson! Jesus said "Have faith in God, for verily I say unto you, if any one of you shall say to this mountain, 'be thou removed and be thou cast into the sea, and shall not doubt in his heart, but shall believe that those things which he saith shall come to pass, he shall have whatsoever he saith."

Then He repeats the lesson. "Therefore, I say unto you, what things so ever you desire, when you pray, believe that you receive them and you shall have them!" (MK. 11:12-24) These are awesome words! Now when did Jesus tell us to believe? Did He say when you see, believe? Did He say when you hear a voice of thunder, believe? No! He said, "WHEN YOU PRAY, BELIEVE YOU RECEIVE." When you pray! When you first ask, believe that you already have it and you will have it! This is the key! This is the secret! When you pray for a thing, believe that you already have it! You do not wait to see! You believe before you see! You believe when you pray!

Now what actually happened when Jesus cursed the fig tree? Although nothing happened that you could see, something happened! The root of the tree began to die! How do we know? Because the Bible said it withered from the root up! The root, the part that you could not see, began to die! Death did not spread up the trunk and into the leaves until the next day. Perhaps it was a week before it was completely dead. But the root began to die the moment Jesus spoke to it!

Now here is how you can receive your miracle! When you pray, believe that you are already healed! The fever may not go down right away, the lump may not disappear instantly, the pain may not stop suddenly, but believe that the root of your sickness is dying! Believe that the root of your problem is dying! Believe it is done and it will be done!

Our problem is that if we rolled someone in the church, in a wheelchair and prayed for them, we would all watch to see if they got up and walked. If they did no get up and walk, we would not believe that they were healed. But the fact is, someone has to believe that they are healed, before we will ever see them get up an walk! I had this very thing happen in one of my meetings. A young lady had been in an automobile accident and was in a wheelchair for five years. She was a lovely lady and had won the pageant, Miss Wheelchair America! She was Miss America in a wheelchair! I was in Revival at a Pentecostal church and her Pastor, who pastored a large Baptist church, called and said he wanted to bring her for prayer.

That night, the Pastor and about forty of his members brought this young lady. After I preached, I had a prayer line. When this lady was rolled up to me in her wheelchair, I put my hands on her head and spoke healing to her. She raised her hands and began rejoicing. But she did not get up and walk. They rolled her out, the same way they rolled her in. But the revival went on for four weeks! So I was still there, when her healing came! Three weeks after I prayed for her, at twelve noon, one day, alone in her kitchen, the

Spirit spoke to her and told her she could now walk! She got up and walked for the first time in five years! She came back to the revival and gave her testimony! Now you see, everyone believed she was healed when they saw her walk, but I believed it three weeks before I saw it! I believed it the night I laid hands on her! Someone has to believe before they see, if we are going to get a miracle!

I do not know if Thomas was ever married, but he seems to have many relatives in the church today. When the Disciples told Thomas that Jesus was alive, he replied that unless he could see Jesus and touch the scars in His Hands, he would not believe. When Thomas saw Jesus and touched the scars, he fell on his face crying "My Lord and My God." Jesus did not say, "Great is thy faith." Instead, He said, "Thomas, you believe in me, because you have seen. But I say unto you, Blessed are they who believe and have not seen!" (Jn. 20:29) That is an awesome statement! You are blessed if you can believe when you have not seen! We walk by Faith and not by sight! Faith is not seeing! Faith is believing what you have no visible evidence of, whatsoever!

FAITH IS NOT FEELING

The second thing I want to tell you is that faith is not feeling.

Now I would not give you a dime for a Faith that did not have feeling. I thank God that we can feel and know that we are saved! We can feel the Spirit and Presence of God! We can feel the joy of knowing Him and serving Him! But I am convinced that people fail in their faith, because they try to walk by feelings. If you ask some people how they know they are saved, they will say that they felt something like hot ants crawling down their back, when they got saved. But what will they do when the ants turn cold? Or they will say they felt warm honey flow over them. But what will they do when it turns to cold molasses? And it will! You see, I know that I am saved, because the Word says that if I believe on the Lord Jesus Christ, I am saved! So I am saved! I do not always feel it, but I am saved! You may see me now, with the presence of God all around me and you know that I have the Joy of a saved person. But I do not always feel the presence of God. Sometimes, it feels that God is a million miles away. But I want you to know that I am saved! Sometimes you may see me with a bowed down head and a tear in my eye. But I am still saved! You see, I am not saved by feelings. I am saved by Faith!

We look too much for feelings. The Bible says if any among you are sick, let him call for the Elders of the church and let them anoint him with oil and pray over him and the prayer of Faith will heal him and the Lord will raise him up! (Jas. 5:17) So what do we do? We call for the sick to come forward. We get the Elders around and pray. But what happens? The people say, "Well, I did not feel anything, so I did not get healed"! This is amazing! The Word did not say if you feel electricity running over you, or if you get knocked down in the floor, you would be healed! It did not say if you feel a bolt from the blue, you will be healed! It says, "The prayer of FAITH will save the sick!" It is not what you feel, it is what you believe that counts!

We have more faith in two aspirin than we do in the Word of God! We get a headache and we take two aspirin.

15

Now what do we feel? Do we feel the aspirin go down and land in our stomach and then little vibrations go up toward our head and then some great force knocks the headache out of us? Of course not! We do not feel anything! We could not tell if the aspirin landed on the left side or the right side. But an hour or so later, the pain goes away! We say, "Well Bayer does work wonders!"

Now can you not see that this is how faith works. We do not feel the pain get knocked out of our arm or foot. We simply believe and the pain goes away!

Several years ago, a lady heard me on the radio. She had been to a number of doctors and had been prayed for, by a number of Ministers. She had been given up to die. Each time she had been for prayer, she expected to feel some mystical power, come and knock her sickness away. But she felt nothing and therefore, doubted her healing. In my message on the radio, I quoted a little poem written by Martin Luther, hundreds of years ago. "Feelings come and feelings go and feelings are deceiving. My faith is in the Word of God, naught else is worth believing." When she heard that little poem, she realized that she did not need to feel something. She needed to believe something! She was healed! She is still healed today!

I had a lady come in one of my prayer lines. She told me that she had been to a number of great Ministers for prayer and she named them. She said none of them had helped her and she came to see if I could help her! I told her I could not help her! She wanted to know why. I told her that she was looking for some Minister who had some magical power that would just come rushing through her and take every symptom away and that there was no need for me to pray for her, because she had been prayed for, by the greatest Preachers in America! She left somewhat upset with me! But the next night she came back. When she came up to me in the prayer line, she told me that what I had said to her, at first made her mad! But then she had stayed awake all night, thinking about it. She said, "Tonight, I did not come to see if you could do anything for me, I came to get healed!" Then she ran around the building! I never touched her! She was healed! Faith is not feeling! Faith is believing what you have not seen of felt!

FAITH IS BELIEVING THE WORD

So Faith is not seeing and faith is not feeling, but what is faith? Faith is believing the Word of God, in spite of everything else to the contrary! But people will say that they believe every word in the Bible! If that is true, then they must believe that they are healed! If you believe every word in the Scriptures, then you must believe that you are healed, regardless of anything to the contrary! The Word does not say that you can be healed or that you should be healed. The Word says that you are healed! Matthew 8:17 says that Jesus Himself, took our infirmities and bore our sicknesses! Isaiah 53:5 says "With His stripes we ARE (right now) healed". First Peter, 2:24 tells us that by His stripes we WERE (Past tense) healed!

Some of the greatest teaching on Faith is found in the fourth chapter of Romans! Look at the the sixteenth verse: "Therefore, it is of Faith that it might be by Grace, to the end, the promise might be sure to all the seed. Not to that only which is of the law, but to that also which is of the Faith of Abraham, who is the father of us all."

Here you see that the promises of God are not only to those who keep the law, but also to those who have Faith! You see, the promises that God gave Abraham were also given to his seed. Now I am not Abraham's heir, by keeping the law. I do not keep the law. But I am his heir, by Faith! So I have the same promises that God gave Abraham! But I must take them by Faith! Now look at the seventeenth verse: "(As it is written, I have made thee a father of many nations) before Him, Whom he believed, even God, Who guickeneth the dead and calleth those things which be not as though they were."

Do you see that God said to Abraham, "I HAVE MADE THEE A FATHER OF MANY NATIONS!" He did not say, "I am going to make you a father." Long before Abraham had any children, God said, "I have MADE you a father." Now I ask you, can God lie? Of course not! But here it says that God calls those things that be not as though they were! Now God called Abraham a father. What was Abraham supposed to call himself? You see, God calls you HEALED, but what are you supposed to call yourself?

Now look at the next verse: "Who against hope, believed in hope, that he might become the father of many nations, according to that which was spoken, 'So shall thy seed be.'" You see, Abraham believed, in spite of everything to the contrary!

Now look at the next two verses: "And being not weak in faith, he considered not his own body, now dead, when he was about an hundred years old, neither yet the deadness of Sarah's womb. He staggered not at the promise of God, through unbelief, but was strong in faith, giving Glory to God."

Many, many people today, can not receive their healing, because they are giving too much attention and consideration to the condition of their own bodies! Think what would happen if Abraham and Sarah were here today and they went to the best Gynecologist of our day. See them walk into the office. The good doctor says, "May I help you?"

"Yes, we want to have a baby."

"You want what?"

"We want to have a baby."

"How old are you sir?"

"I will be a hundred years old my next birthday."

"How old are you maam?"

"1 was ninety years old my last birthday."

Now what would the doctor say? He would tell them to go play with someone else's grandchild! In other words, it is impossible! Yet Abraham and Sarah believed what God said!

Today, sick people can tell you what the Gynecologist said, what the Cardiologist said, what the Radiologist said, what uncle John said or what aunt Sally said. But they can not tell you what God Said! But God Said that Jesus Himself, bore your sicknesses and with His stripes, you are healed!

But how can you get this kind of faith? How can you come to the place that you just believe God, no matter what you see or feel or hear? Well, how did Abraham do it? Look at the next verse: "And being fully persuaded, that what God had promised, He was able also to perform.!

Do you see that? Abraham was fully persuaded that God was able to do what He had promised! Are you fully persuaded? Are you totally convinced that God can not lie? I am! I am fully persuaded and convinced that God can and will do exactly what He has promised!

My Wife and I can identify with Abraham and Sarah. After we had been married six years, my wife was told by three Gynecologists that she could never have a child. They said she had juvenile womb. Her womb had never developed from a child!

We wanted children We picked out names for our children before we were ever married! We said we would have a girl and name her Camelia and call her Camy. We would have a boy and call him Randall. But now, the Doctors were telling us that we can never have a child! We prayed and sought God. We decided to stand on the Word, "If two of you shall agree on earth as touching anything they shall ask, it shall be done for them of my Father in Heaven." (MAT.18:19) When my wife became pregnant, we went back to the same three doctors. They had her come back the next day for more tests. They said, "Mrs. Hunt, we do not understand it, but you are going to have a baby." When our daughter was born, the delivering doctor told people in the hallways, that this was a Miracle baby! He was as excited as we were. Three years later we prayed and agreed again that God would give us a boy. Today, we have a Girl named Camelia and we call her Camy! We have a Boy named Randall!

They each have a boy and a girl, so we have four wonderful Grandchildren! We believed God, in spite of everything to the contrary!

I am not kicking Doctors or medicine. I believe in both. I have a number of close friends who are Doctors. I work very close with several doctors, in my counseling Ministry.

But the problem is that people make a god out of the Doctors. If I were in your town or church preaching and you went out and invited people to come, you would hear many say that they can not come because they are sick! If you told them to come on, because this man prays for the sick, they would tell you that they are not able to go and sit for several hours in the service. Yet if the Doctor told these same people to go to a Regional Hospital in another city, some miles away, they would get up the next morning at four o'clock and drive to the hospital to be there at seven. Then they would sit there until three in the afternoon, waiting for the Doctor, or the test, or the results! When will you let God be your God? He is my Savior, and my Healer!

Many years ago, a teenage girl was given up to die, with cancer. She was given just a few weeks to live. Her mother talked to her about getting ready for Heaven. She accepted Jesus as her Saviour. She lay there on her bed, reading the Bible, one day, when she said, excitedly, "Mama, did you know that the Bible says I am healed? Get my shoes, I want to get up!" Her mother tried to still her and told her that she must lay still. She was told that she only had a few weeks and that the family wanted her to stay here as long as possible. She Said, "NO mama, no, the Bible says I am healed! I want to get up!" Again her mother tried to talk her out of it. The Girl replied, "Mama, you told me to believe what this Word says and it says I am healed! Get my shoes, I want to get up!" Her mother got her shoes and she got up! Today, she is over sixty years old and is preaching the Gospel!

Your feet should be shod with the shoes of the preparation of the Gospel of peace! Now, get your shoes on! Get up! Believe God! You have been made whole!

CHAPTER 2

HOW FAITH WORKS

Now that we know what faith is, let us find out how faith works. People often say to me, "Do you mean that if I just believe a thing, it is so?" Yes! That is exactly what I am saying! "Whatsoever you shall ask in faith, believing, you shall receive." (Mt. 21:22)

"Do you mean to tell me that if I believe I am saved, I am saved?" Yes! That is exactly what I am saying! "Believe on the Lord Jesus Christ and you shall be saved." (Acts 16:31)

"Do you mean to tell me that if I believe I am healed, I am healed?" Yes! That is exactly what I am saying!

"If you shall ask anything in my name believing, you shall receive." (Jn. 14:14) "The Prayer of Faith shall save the sick and the Lord shall raise him up." (Jas. 5:15) "By His stripes, you were healed" (1 Pet. 2:23)

This seems so incredible to some people. How can it be, that if I just believe, a thing is done? It is amazing, that God has already provided everything we will ever need and all we have to do is believe! God did all the hard part! He gave His Son and let Him take our sins, our sicknesses and our sorrows! He took them all in our place, then died to pay the price for all of them, then rose from the dead, to become the High Priest of our Faith! (Heb. 3:1) Then God gave us the easy parts Just believe! "Believe that you already have it and you shall have it." (Mk. 11:24)

How can this be? The best way that I know to illustrate to you, how faith works, is to use a Radio or Television. You see these things work by waves that you can not see or feel!

I have been on a number of Radio and TV stations, so I understand a little about it. When I talk into a microphone at a Radio station, my words go into a transformer. This transformer, transforms my words into radio waves. These are sent to a transmitter, which sends them to a tower and the waves are sent out, all over the area. Now, in your house, you have what we now call a radio. But in reality, it is a radio receiver. It receives radio waves. In this receiver, there is a transformer that transforms the waves, back into sound, so that you hear what I am saying at the station. You can not stand outside the tower and hear it, because you can not hear the radio waves! You can only hear it, when it is converted back into sound!

You see, there are sounds and pictures around you right now, no matter where you are! You do not hear them or feel them or see them, but they are there! If you simply turn on your radio or television, you will hear the sounds and see the pictures. Your radio and your TV are your receivers! They do not bring the waves into your house! The waves are already there! The receivers simply pick up the waves and convert them back into sounds and pictures!

Now suppose I am on the radio and you want to hear my program. You call and ask me if I am on the radio and I tell you that I am. You tell me you want the program sent to your house. I would tell you, "It is there, turn your radio on." Then you say, "Well I do not hear it." I would say, "Turn your radio on." You then say, "Well I do not see it or feel it." I would again say, "Turn your radio on."

Now this may all sound silly, but I am making a point. No matter how much you wanted to hear my program, no matter how long you waited for it, no matter how much you argued with me about it, you would never receive it, until you turned your receiver on! The program has been made. It has been converted to waves. It has been sent out (transmitted) all over the area! But you will only hear it, by using a receiver (radio)!

JESUS IS THE ANNOUNCER

Now let us apply this to the Word! Do you understand that Jesus came to bring Salvation, Deliverance, Healing, Love, Joy, Peace, Prosperity, and everything else that mankind needs! Jesus paid the total price for us to have all these things! So from the cross, there was broadcast everything that you and I need! Jesus saved, forgave sins, healed, delivered, cast out demons, and set men free! But while Jesus was on earth, He was human. He was one man in one place at the time. He was limited by His humanity as to how many people he could touch at one time! So after He rose from the dead, He ascended back to the Father. But He said He would send another Comforter! And He sent back the Holy Spirit! Now the Holy Spirit is everywhere at the same time, all the time! Everything that Jesus came to bring us, has been converted into the Holy Spirit! It really has! So every person who gets saved, gets saved by the Holy Spirit! Every person who gets healed, gets healed by the Holy Spirit! In other words, everything that God is doing today, He is doing through and by the Holy Spirit!

24

Can you see it now? Jesus came and paid the price for every need of mankind. Then He ascended to Heaven and sent back the Holy Spirit with everything we need! So Jesus is the announcer and the Holy Spirit is the radio wave! While Jesus could only be in one place at a time, when He was here on earth, The Holy Spirit is everywhere all the time!

FAITH IS THE RECEIVER

So Jesus is the broadcaster (announcer) and the Holy Spirit is the radio wave. But we now need a receiver. We have one! The Bible tells us that God has given to EVERY MAN the measure of faith! (Rom. 12:3) Not A measure, but THE measure! What measure? The Measure that is needed to receive your miracle! This Measure of faith is your receiver! You need to turn it on! When you turn your faith on, it simply puts you in touch with the Holy Spirit! You are in the Spirit! Now your faith receives the Spirit and simply converts it back into your miracle! It is that simple! Never say that you do not have faith. You do have it. God has given it to you!

When you pray, turn your faith on. You will sense that you are in the Spirit. Remember, the Spirit is your healing, your deliverance, your miracle! Believe it and receive it! You felt the Spirit, now let your faith convert that into your Miracle! I have prayed for people who have said, "I really felt the Spirit and got a good blessing, but I did not get my healing." To me that is incredible. Is there one Spirit that blesses us and shouts us and dances us, and then another Spirit that heals us? Of course not! There are many gifts, many ministries, many manifestations, many miracles, but

25

all by the Same Spirit! (1 Cor. 12:4-6) The same Holy Ghost that blesses you is the One Who heals you!

Now do you understand that when people are listening to the radio, a person on one side of town does not have to wait until someone on the other side of town turns their radio off, in order to listen? They can all listen at the same time! The announcer is in the station, but the radio wave is all over the area! So it is with the Spirit. You and I and a thousand other people, all over the world, can turn our faith on at the same time and receive the Spirit. He is everywhere! Each of us who turn on our faith will receive the Same Spirit, but our faith will convert Him into our individual needs! So one may receive Him and be saved, while another receives Him and is healed, at the same time! According to your faith, so be it unto you! (Mt. 9:29)

HOW TO TURN ON YOUR FAITH

Now what have we learned? We have learned that Jesus bore our sins, our sicknesses and our sorrows. He paid the price and bought our salvation, our healing and our deliverance. Because He was in the flesh and could only be in one place at the time, He ascended to Heaven and transformed our needs into the Holy Spirit. He sent back the Holy Spirit with every thing that we need. He gave us a receiver, which is our measure of faith.

When we turn on our faith, we are in touch with the Spirit. Our faith then transforms the Spirit into our miracle. That's it! It works!

Now the question is how do we turn on our faith? Faith comes by hearing the Word. (Rom. 10:17) When we hear the Promises of God, we need to believe that they are true and that they are to us, personally! We must take some action that seals our faith! The best way to do this is by making what has been called, 'a point of contact.' What is a point of contact? It is some action that we do, that when we do it, we will never again doubt that we have received our miracle! No matter what happens! No matter what we feel or see, we will never again doubt that we have received our miracle!

A point of contact can be anything we choose! We can draw a chalk line in the floor and say, "When I step over this line, I will be healed!" We step over the line and from that moment on, we believe that we are healed, no matter what happens! We can use the Minister's hands. We can say, "When this man touches me, I am going to accept my healing." His hands are laid on us and no matter what we feel or see, we believe we are healed from that moment on! Never again to doubt!

This works so perfectly that it will even work with someone who is not a true man or woman of God! This is how some people who are not genuine, go about preaching and claiming to be Ministers and still have miracles take place in their services! This may not seem right, but it happens. Here is why! Suppose I am a false preacher, but you do not know that I am a false preacher. And suppose you come to my meeting and you say in your heart, "Lord, when that man lays hands on me, I am going to believe for my healing." Then I lay hands on you and you turn your faith on. You receive your Miracle! Not because of who or what I am, but because of your faith! You see, no matter where you are or who is present, any time you turn your faith on, you are in touch with the Holy Spirit! He is everywhere! Your faith transforms Him into your Miracle!

You see, this will work with a pine tree! Suppose you decide to use a pine tree as your point of contact. Now we know the tree has no anointing. It is neither righteous nor unrighteous. It is just a tree. But if you say, "When I touch this tree, I will be made whole" and you touch the tree and turn on your faith, you will receive your miracle!

The problem today is that if you told some preachers that you touched that tree and received a miracle, they would cut the tree down and cut it into little pieces. Then they would put your picture in a magazine and send it all over the nation. They would tell how you touched the tree and got healed. Then they would offer to send a chip off the tree, to everyone who sent them five dollars!

Now think, if you read the article and sent the five dollars and got the chip of the tree and you touch the chip and turned your faith on, you would still receive a miracle! Not because of the Minister. Not because of the five dollars. Not because of the chip! But because you turned on your faith! You believed and your faith made you whole!

On the other hand, if you are looking for some magic in the chip, you could wear it around your neck or sprinkle salt and pepper on it and eat it and it would still do you no good! It is your Faith that saves you! It is your faith that heals you! It is your Faith that gets your prayers answered. And God has given you that measure of faith!

Now, suppose you call God and you ask Him if He is still doing miracles today and He tells you He is. Now you tell Him you want a miracle sent to you. He would say, "It is there, turn your faith on." You say, "But I do not see it or feel it." He would say, "Turn your faith on." You may get angry or you may pray until you are blue in the face, but you will not receive the Miracle until you turn on your Faith!

I had a business man come to me for prayer. He had a heart condition and had to take tablets when he felt the pain. He told me he had been prayed for a number of times and he would get better for a while, then the pain would return. I told him he had been pulling up the stake. He did not understand, so I told him, he needed to make a point of contact, drive down a stake and never doubt his healing again! I told him to take our a pen and paper. He did. I told him to write down the date and time. He did. I then told him to write, "This night at this time, God healed me." He wrote it all down and went away rejoicing. I saw him two years later. He told me this story: "I went for over a year and had no symptoms whatsoever. Then one day on the job, I felt the pain. My first thought was to run home and get a pill. I started to my truck, but just as soon as I sat down I thought about that piece of paper. I pulled it out of my wallet and read it. As soon as I read it, I felt the Spirit. I have not had another pain! I am healed!"

DOES THE BIBLE TEACH THIS

Now I know all of this may sound strange, but it is what the Word teaches! Look in the fifth chapter of Mark, beginning with the twenty-fourth verse. It tells of a woman who had an issue of blood for twelve years and had spent all she had on doctors and was still not better, but worse. Jesus is walking down the road with a great crowd of people following Him. She heard of His coming and she made herself a point of contact! She said, "If I can just touch the hem of His garment, I shall be made whole." Now she had never seen or heard of anyone else doing this. This was her point of contact! She actually had to get down and crawl, because the crowd was so great. As Jesus passed by, she stretched forth her hand and His garment just brushed her hand. She was healed!

Now if she had been like some of us, she would have said, "Oh I did not get a good hold on it". You see, some people would not believe it they were sitting in His lap. But she set her point of contact and she turned her faith on! She got her miracle! Now what did Jesus say to her? Did He say, "Daughter my miracle anointed garment has made you whole"? It was not His garment that healed her! When he asked who had touched Him, the Disciples told him that the multitude was thronging Him. If it had been His garment, then people would have been falling out all up and down the road. But out of all that touched Him, the only one who received a miracle was the one who said, "When I touch Him, I will be made whole".

Did Jesus say that His garment had made her whole? Did He say that some Angel standing beside Him had made her whole? No. He said, "Daughter, THY FAITH hath made thee whole"! It was her faith. She made a point of contact. She turned on her faith. She got in touch with the Spirit. She was healed!

Let us review what we have learned. Jesus bought and paid for everything that we need. He ascended to Heaven and sent back The Holy Spirit with all of our needs. He gave us a measure of faith which is our receiver. When we turn on our receiver, we are in touch with the Holy Spirit. Our Faith transforms the Spirit into our miracle! We use a point of contact to turn our faith on! God will directly respond to our faith! When you pray, believe that you have received and you shall have! Right now, make yourself a point of contact! Write it down! Write down the date and time! Act on your faith! Touch your point of contact! Now turn your faith on! Never again doubt that you have received a miracle!

CHAPTER 3

THE STEPS OF FAITH

Now we know what faith is and we know how faith works! I want to give you precise steps to take, to receive your miracle! There are three exact steps to take to receive a miracle. I want you to learn them and use them. They really do work!

STEP 1:
BELIEVE THAT YOU HAVE RECEIVED

The very first step is to believe that you have received! I did not say, 'believe that you ARE GOING to receive'! I did not say, 'believe that you OUGHT TO receive'! I said, "Believe that you HAVE (ALREADY) received'! Again I remind you that Jesus said, "When you pray, believe that you receive". (Mk. 11:24) This is the missing key in most people's faith! You must believe that you have it and you will get it! You must believe that you already have it, in spite of anything else to the contrary! No matter what you see. No matter what you feel. No matter what the circumstances might be. You must hold on to your faith! Let me give you several examples.

A lady was brought to one of my services, who had stomach cancer. She had been under doctor's care. She was brought from the hospital to the service. The doctors had given her radium and cobalt treatments. Now they had scheduled her for surgery on the following Monday, to remove part of her stomach. She came to my service of Thursday night, before her scheduled surgery. I laid hands on her and prayed. She fell on the floor. People who knew her came up and started fanning her, because she had been fed, intravenously for the past several days and they thought she was too weak to stand. I told them that God was performing a miracle on her. When she got up, she testified that God had healed her!

She returned to the hospital and told her doctor that God had healed her! The doctor had x-rays done and showed her on the xray that there was a big, white spot and told her the cancer was still there and they must operate.

Now here is where most of us would have stumbled. When we saw the x-ray, we would assume that we were wrong about our healing. But not this lady! She said, "Doctor, it does not matter what the x-ray shows, God healed me Thursday night". They put her to sleep and cut into her. When they got into her stomach, the cancer was gone! There was a scar, where it had been and no doubt, that was what showed up on the x-ray. When she woke up, the Doctor came in and told her that they found no cancer and his next words were, "I guess that cobalt did the trick after all". She replied, "Cobalt my foot! I told you that God healed me Thursday night'!

Now here is where real faith comes in. This lady had to believe that she was already healed, regardless of what the x-ray showed! On another occasion, I prayed for a woman who had arthritis in her hands and fingers. She suffered much pain for several years, before I prayed for her. After prayer, her pain and swelling left. She went for several months without pain. Then one day, she was hanging out wet clothes. It was a chilly day. Suddenly her fingers began to ache. Now She could have said, "Oh no! The arthritis is coming back!" But instead, she said, "I wonder what that is. I know it is not arthritis, because God has healed me of that." Immediately, the pain left and she has been healed ever since! Do you see how you must believe, no matter what you see or feel? You must believe that you Have received! Since I have already covered much about believing, I want to take you to the second step of faith.

STEP 2:
CONFESS WITH YOUR MOUTH

The second step of faith is to confess with your mouth, what you believe in your heart. I think most people do not realize how much the Bible teaches about confessing faith. When I first began teaching on confessing faith, years ago, I ran into much opposition about it. People would say, "Brother I do not want to tell a lie. I do not want to say I am healed, if I am not." Now I know these people were sincere. But I also know they were unlearned about what the Scripture teaches. Nothing is received from God, until one confesses it! The Bible says, "If thou shalt confess with thy mouth, the Lord Jesus Christ and shalt believe in thine heart that God has raised Him from the dead, thou shalt be saved. For with the heart man believeth unto Righteousness, but with the Mouth, Confession Is Made Unto Salvation." (Rom. 10:9-10)

You see, you are not even saved, until you say so! That is why the Bible says, "Let the redeemed of the Lord SAY SO." (Ps. 107:2)

Now look at this word, salvation. It comes from the Greek word, SOZO. It means to be made whole, body, mind, soul and spirit. So if confession is made unto SOZO with the mouth, then you are only saved when you say so! You are only healed when you say so! You are only free when you say so! You do not receive it until you confess it with your mouth! You must believe in your heart that you already have it and you must confess with your mouth that you already have it!

This is not lying. This is letting the words of your mouth agree with the Word of God! This is why the Bible says, "Let the weak say, 'I am strong'." (Joel 3:10) Are the weak lying? When the Bible says that God calls those things which be not as though they were, (Rom. 4:17) is God lying? Of course not. The fact is that Satan is a liar and the father of lies. Now if Satan is the father of lies, then all his children are lies! So whatever Satan comes up with, to hurt or destroy you, is a lie! God says He has redeemed you! God says He has healed you! God says He has delivered you! God says He has supplied all of your needs! He says He did all of this when He hung His Son, Jesus on the Cross! This is what the Word of God says! Now the Word also says, Let every thing else be a liar! Let God be true! (Rom. 3:4)

God changes people and things, by changing their names. Long before Abram had a child, God named him, "Father of Many Nations." Long before Jacob became a true Prince of God, God named him Israel. (Prince of God) When God changed these and other people's names, what were the people supposed to call themselves? They were supposed to let their confession agree with what God said! They were supposed to call themselves, what God called them!

Now God calls you saved, healed, delivered, victorious, overcoming, prosperous, and a number of other good things! But what are you calling yourself? Let your confession agree with what the Word of God says! Let God be true!

The Bible says that Jesus is the High Priest of our confession! (Heb. 3:1) What does this mean? It means that Christ acts on what we profess to have! He can only act on our confession! He can only give us what we profess to have or confess that we have!

Now this is important! Christ can only give us what we say we have! What if we continue to say, "I am lost. I am not saved. I do not feel saved. I still have the urges and symptoms of sin in my life, so I am not going to confess that I am saved, because I do not want to tell a lie." Can we ever be saved, without confessing that we are saved? No! Jesus can only save us, when we say we are saved through His Blood!

He is the High Priest of our confession. He wants to act in our behalf, but He is waiting for us to confess that we have what His Word declares that we have! Now what if we continue to confess, "I am not healed. I do not feel healed. I still have the pains and symptoms of sickness in my body, so I am not going to confess that I am healed. I do not want to tell a lie." Can we ever be healed without confessing that we are healed? No! We must profess to have what the Word says we have, so that the High Priest of our confession, can act on our profession. With the mouth, confession is made unto SOZO! With the mouth, confession is made unto salvation, healing, deliverance and anything else that the Word promises us!

Do not be afraid to take this step of faith. After all, you have nothing to lose, by letting the words of your mouth agree with the Word of God! Profess, with your mouth, to have what the Word says you have!

STEP 3:
ACT ON YOUR FAITH

The third step I want to teach you, is to act on your faith! In the Book of James, we are told that Faith without works is dead. (Jas. 2:20) Many people think that James and Paul had a disagreement, because Paul said we do not receive the blessings by works but by faith. Then James said that faith without works is dead. But there is no conflict here. Paul is talking about works of Righteousness, which will get us nothing. But James is talking about works of faith. James' word could have been and probably should have been trans-lated "actions'. Thus we would read, "Faith without actions is dead". This is so true. James goes on to say, "Show me thy faith without (actions) and I will show you my faith by my (actions)! (Jas. 2:18) In other words, we must not just believe and confess. We must also act on our faith!

Jesus had people to do this time after time.

Once there was a man in the temple who had a withered hand. Now this was not just a paralyzed hand. It was a small, withered thing, just hanging there. Jesus told him to "Stretch forth thy hand." (Mk. 3:1-5) Now the man could have said, "I can not move my hand. You see it is deformed. I can not stretch it forth." But instead, he no doubt thought, "I will try." He tried! He acted on his faith! The hand and arm grew out just as long and as big as the other one!

Jesus found a man, who had lain on his bed for thirty eight years. Jesus told him to "Rise, take up thy bed and walk." (Jn. 5:4-7) The man could have protested, "I have lain here for thirty eight years. If I could get up, don't you know that I would? I am crippled. I can not walk." But instead, he no doubt thought, "I will try." He tried to move and he moved! He tried to stand and he stood! He tried to pick up his bed and he picked it up! He tried to walk and he walked! Over and over in the Bible, God requires people to act on their faith! In fact, it is hard to think of any miracle in the Bible, where a person was not required to act on their faith!

I once met a man, who was in a wheel chair. He had been there for many years and was on disability! I prayed for him and talked to him about faith. He ask his family to get two, one-gallon paint buckets and fill them with sand. These two buckets of sand were placed on each side of his chair, with the handles up. He began to tell himself that he would pick up those buckets of sand and walk. Each day he would hook his fingers through the handles and try to lift them. At first, he could only hook his fingers in the handles, because he was totally paralyzed. But he continued to believe that he was healed. Gradually he got to where he could pull on the buckets, then lift them, then raise them over his head! In a few months, he got out of the wheelchair and walked with the two buckets of sand! Now this is a true story! It really did happen! I am a witness to it. He actually had to give up his disability and go back to work! But he was glad to do so! He was healed!

Many years ago, when I was still a boy at my mothers home, I had pneumonia. I lay on the bed for four days, hurting, aching, running a high fever and begging God to heal me! On the fifth day, I looked up into the ceiling and said,

"God why don't you heal me?' As if He spoke out of the ceiling, God said, "Why don't you believe?" It upset me! I thought, "Well I will show you that I believe." I got up, still aching and put on my clothes. I started out the door. I was going to walk to town, which was about a half mile away. There was snow on the ground. My Sister asked where I was going. I told her I was going up town. She told me I would catch my death if I went outside! I told her I was already dying and I was going to catch my life! I do not know exactly when it happened. I had gone several blocks, when suddenly I noticed I could breathe freely. The fever left! The pain left! I was healed and I have never had pneumonia again! I have learned, through the years, to always act on my faith!

If you can not raise your hand, try raising it! You have nothing to lose! If you can not bend your back, try bending it! If you can not eat certain foods, try eating them! Believe that you are healed! Confess that you are healed! Act as if you are healed! I learned that God is pleased when I believe His word, confess His Word and act on His Word! I could give you many, many examples of people receiving miracles by taking these three steps There was a lady who came in my prayer line, who said her favorite food was a cola and a hamburger, but she could not eat these things, because she had ulcers. She said that every time she came to church, she had to come by her favorite hamburger place and it was a struggle not to stop. I told her that God had healed her and I wanted her to believe that and confess that! I then told her that I wanted her to go, after church and get her a cola and hamburger! The next night she came back and testified that she had done what I had told her and that today, she had eaten three hamburgers and drank three drinks and there was no pain! Everyone had a good laugh, when I told her not to over do it, but to continue acting on her faith.

I can not emphasize this enough! Faith without corresponding actions is dead! It is not enough to believe it! It is not enough to speak it! You must also act on it! When a person believes on the Lord and confesses their salvation, it also behooves them to act as if they are saved! Their lifestyle must change! Their habits must change! They must act like they are saved!

So it is with anything you seek from God. You must believe that you have received it! You must confess that you have received it! And you must act as if you have received it! These are the steps of Faith that will bring a Miracle into your life!

CHAPTER 4

THE NAME OF JESUS

We now know what faith is. We know how it works. We know the steps of faith. But how do we know it will work for us, or how do I know it will work for me? This is the question that plagues most people. They think, "I know what the Bible says that God will do, but how do I know He will do it for me? I may not be good enough. I may have done something that will prevent me from receiving. How do I know?" To add to this, Satan is always the accuser of the Saints. He is ever telling us how unworthy we are. He reminds us of how little we have done for God or how much we have failed. So how can I ever be sure that I will receive a miracle?

There is an answer to these questions! It is a wonderful answer! It is so wonderful that it is almost incomprehensible! It is the fact that we can use the Name of Jesus!

I want to show you the very words of Jesus in John, 14:12-14: "Verily, verily I say unto you, He that believeth on me, the works that I do, shall he do also. And greater works than these shall he do, because I go to my Father. And whatsoever ye shall ask the Father in my Name, that will I do, that the Father may be glorified in the Son. If ye shall ask anything in my Name, I will do it."

I remember when this Scripture was revealed into my spirit. All my Christian life, I had always ended my prayers with, "in Jesus' Name, amen" But I never knew why. I did it because that is what I heard other people do. Then one day, I was in an extended fast.   After a number of days of fasting, God Spoke to me! He told me to go back and read the New Testament as if I had never read it before. Then He stopped me! He said, "Do not read into it, what you have been taught. Read out of it, what it says." Now this was amazing! Do you realize how often we read the Scripture and simply read into it, what we have been taught? Sadly, if we find a scripture that contradicts our religion or doctrine, we simply pass over it as if it is not there! To read the Bible and let it say what it says, whether it agrees with our doctrine or not, is a wonderful thing!

So, in obedience to what God had spoken to me, I began to read the New Testament for the fortieth time! You see, I was an avid Bible reader! I had already read the Bible through, thirteen times and the New Testament, thirty nine times, in my first dozen years as a Christian! Now I was reading the New Testament for the fortieth time! But God wanted me to read it as if I had never read it before! He evidently had something He wanted to show me!

I was reading along and came to John, 14:12. The Spirit stopped me there! He would not let me go on! He spoke to me! The conversation went like this:

Holy Spirit: "What does this say?"

Me: "It says that believers can do the same works that Jesus did."

"What did Jesus do?'

"He healed the sick, He performed miracles."

"Are you a believer?"

"Yes I am."

"Can you heal the sick?"

"No I can not."

"You do not believe my Word."

I was astonished! What was the Spirit saying to me? For many days, I stayed right there on this Scripture! The conversation repeated itself over and over:

"What does it say?"

"It says that Believers can do the same works that Jesus did."

"What did Jesus do?"

"He worked Miracles."

"Are you a believer?"

"Yes I am."

"Can you work a miracle?"

"No I can not."

"You do not believe my Word."

Now what was my problem? I was not doubting God! I was doubting myself! You see, I believed that God would do miracles for a number of Great people that I knew, but I could not believe He would do it for me! I was a nobody. I did not live good enough. I was not holy enough. I could think of a number of reasons why God would not answer my prayers. In fact, THE HARDEST BATTLE I EVER FOUGHT, WAS BELIEVING THAT GOD WOULD DO THE MIRACULOUS FOR ME!

As I said, Satan is ever present to accuse us and cause us to doubt. He will always show us our faults, failures and short comings! It took me days to learn this one thing: God's Word was talking to me, personally! It was not just for the good and perfect. There are no good and perfect! It is for me! It is for you, personally!

When God finally got this through my head and into my spirit, I went and bought me a Giant Print New Testament! I wanted to be able to write between the lines and I could do it in this Giant Print New Testament! I went through the New Testament for the forty first time! Everywhere that I found the words, 'you', 'ye', 'thee' or 'thou', I wrote my name! Now here is how John 14:12-14 reads in my Giant Print New Testament:

Verily, verily I say unto Franklin Hunt, if Franklin Hunt believes in me, the Works that I do, Franklin Hunt shall do also. And greater works than these shall Franklin Hunt do, because I go to my Father, And whatsoever Franklin Hunt shall ask in my name, that will I do that the Father may be glorified in the Son. If Franklin Hunt shall ask anything in my Name I will do it. Now here is a wonderful thing! Jesus has given us the right to use HIS NAME! He has given us the right to go to God the Father, in the Name Of Jesus! He tells us that whatever we ask the Father for, in the Name of Jesus, He will give us! Now I have a weapon against Satan and his accusations! I say, "Devil, for one time in your life you are right! I do not deserve anything God has. I am not good enough. I do not live good enough. But there is one thing you are forgetting Satan. When I go to God, I am not going in my name! I am not going on my righteousness! I am going in the Name Of Jesus! And He is Righteousness! He is perfect! He is Holy! I am going to receive from God, not because of who or what I am, but because of Who Jesus Is!"

Let us go to John 16:24-27:

"Hitherto have ye asked nothing in my Name; ask and ye shall receive that your joy may be full. These things have I spoken to you in proverbs; but the time cometh, when I shall no longer speak unto you in proverbs, but I shall show you plainly of the Father. At that day ye shall ask in my name; and I say not unto you that I will pray the Father for you: For the Father Himself loveth you, because ye have loved me and have believed that I came out from God."

Jesus is saying that, up until now, you have not been asking in my Name. You have simply come to me in person. But I am going away. So I am telling you to start going to the Father and asking in My Name! Whatever you ask the Father in My Name, He will give it to you!

He even goes further and says, that we do not even need to ask Jesus to pray to the Father for us, because the Father Himself loves us, because we have loved Jesus and have believed that He came out from God! Praise God! Can you grasp this? You and me, ordinary people, who have accepted Christ as our Saviour, have the Right to go directly to God Himself and ask for anything in the Name of Jesus and we will receive it!

There are many people who pray to Mary or one of the Saints of old, believing that these Saints will intercede for them, in prayer. They believe that Mary will ask Jesus, and because she is His Mother, He will turn and ask the Father, because He does not want to disappoint His mother! They believe that God will give it to His Son. The Son will give it to His Mother and Mary will give it to us. This all sounds good, But in these Scriptures, Jesus builds a "bypass' around all this! He tells me that I can go directly into the Throne Room! I do not need to go through anyone else! I can go directly to God Himself! And I, who am not worthy of anything, will still receive, because I am not going in my name! I am going in the Name of Jesus! What a wonderful

Name! What a Glorious Name! What a powerful Name! And I have the Right to use it!

THE MILLIONAIRE

To get a clear understanding of this, suppose a Millionaire was to come to you and tell you that he was going on a long trip and that he wanted you to be better off when he returned. Suppose he then handed you a book of blank checks, with His Name signed to each one. Suppose he then told you that if you needed anything while he was gone, to take one of the checks and write it out for the amount you needed and take it to the bank and the teller would give you whatever you wrote the check for! What would you do?

When your bills came due and your car broke down, would you say, "Well I really need some help, but I do not feel worthy to use this man's money." Would you say, "I am not sure he really meant what he said." Perhaps you would say things like that, but not me! When I had a need, I would write a check! I believe I could spend some of that man's money, before he got back!

Now suppose you have no money in the bank. You have very little. You are dressed shabbily. But you write the check and go to the bank. When the Teller sees you, he might think, "Why is this person in this bank? He does not have an account here." But when you lay the check before the teller, he sees that you are not coming in your name. You are not coming on what you have in the bank. You are coming in the Name of a Millionaire, who has much money in that bank! You are going to receive what you wrote the

46

check for, not because of who you are, or what you have, but because you have come in the name of a rich person!

Do you see, that Jesus said He was going away, but He left us a book of blank checks! These checks are the promises in the New Testament and Jesus has signed His Name to everyone of them! Now all we have to do is take one of these promises to The Father, in the Name of Jesus and The Father will give us that promise! We receive because of the Name of Jesus, on that promise!

THE LAWYER

The story is told that a lawyer sat in church one day and heard the Pastor read the above Scriptures. The lawyer stood and asked the Pastor, "Do you mean that Jesus has given us the power of attorney over His business?"

The Pastor replied, "Sir, you are a lawyer, You tell us what it means."

The Lawyer said, "If the Scripture is a legal contract, then in these verses, Christ has given us the power of attorney. We have the right to use His Name. We have the right to conduct His business."

The Pastor said, "Please explain to us, what this means."

The Lawyer answered, "It depends on what is behind the name. When someone gives you power of attorney, they give you the right to use their name, to act in their place. You have the right to handle their business. If they are worth ten thousand dollars, then you have the right to manage, use or spend that ten thousand dollars. If they are worth a million dollars, then you have the right to manage, spend or use that million dollars. So it depends on what is behind the name."

The Pastor then turned and read where Jesus said, "All power in Heaven and earth is given unto me." (Mt. 28-18) The Pastor then asked the Lawyer, "Now what does it mean?"

The Lawyer answered, "It means that we can ask for anything in the Name of Jesus and it will be given to us!"

Now I do not know if this is a true story, but I do know that the analogy is true! We have been given the right to use the Name of Jesus! We have been given the power of attorney! The right to act in His place and to do His business!

Therefore, we can preach and teach in the Name of Jesus and souls will be saved! We can lay hands on the sick in the Name of Jesus and people will be healed! We can cast out devils in the Name of Jesus and demons will flee away! We can pray in the Name of Jesus and prayers will be answered! We have been given the right and authority to use the Name of Jesus!

THE SONG

Charles Wycuff was a friend of mine. He was a great Gospel song writer. He wrote many songs that became top hits in the field of Gospel Music. One of his greatest songs was entitled, "What A Lovely Name." Some of the words of this song were,

"What a Lovely Name the Name of Jesus
Reaching higher far, than the brightest star"

What is he saying?

To fully understand, go outside at night and look up into the sky. The brightest star in the sky is a star called Sirius or commonly known as "The dog star." (Alpha Canis Majoris) Now go and ask an astronomer how far away from us, this star is. The astronomer will tell you that that star is over eight light years away! But tell him that you do not understand light years. He will explain that light travels at the speed of one hundred and eighty six thousand miles per second. Now multiply that by sixty and you will know how far light travels in a minute. Now multiply that by sixty and you will know how far light travels in an hour. Now multiply that by twenty four and you will know how far light travels in a day. Now multiply that by three hundred and sixty five and you will know how far light travels in a year! Now multiply that by eight and seven tenths and you will know how many billions of miles that star is away from us!

Yet in his song, Brother Wycuff is saying that even if there was a devil on that star, I can walk out, look up into the sky and say, "Devil I rebuke you in the Name of Jesus!" And way over there on that star, the devil will bow down!

What a lovely Name! What a powerful Name! What an awesome Name! If what the astronomers tell us is true, then this earth is just one planet in a solar system with eight other planets. This solar system is just one of millions of solar systems in a galaxy called the Milky Way. This galaxy is just one in a universe of millions of galaxies. So I am just one small speck of dust in this universe. Yet the Christ who created this entire universe, has given this small speck of dust (Me), the right to use His Name and conduct His business on this small planet! As incomprehensible as this all sounds, it is true!

THE DECLARATION OF PAUL

Sitting in a prison, thinking about all that Jesus had done for him and all that Jesus had brought him through, Paul, the

Apostle, got excited about the Name of Jesus! He declared, "Wherefore God also hath highly exalted him (Jesus) and given him a name which is above every name. That at the name of Jesus, every knee should bow, of things in heaven and things in earth and things under the earth. And that every tongue should confess that Jesus Christ is Lord, to the Glory of God the Father." (Phil. 2:9-11)

What is Paul saying? He is saying that every knee in Heaven will bow to the Name of Jesus and every knee on earth will bow at The Name of Jesus and every knee in Hell will bow at the Name of Jesus!

Now in our imagination let us ascend to Heaven. Let us walk down the golden streets and see the wondrous sights. Let us hear the praise and adoration going up to God. Let us keep walking until we find Gabriel! That tall, bright Angel who stands at the right hand of God!. That Angel who was chosen to announce the very birth of Jesus! Let us walk up to that Angel and mention the Name of Jesus. That Angel will bow to that name!

Now let us leave Heaven and descend. Down to this earth, down to the grave, down past death, on down to Hell itself. Let us walk around in Hell and hear the screams of the doomed. Let us walk past the different ranks of devils and demons, until we come to Satan himself! That Devil who has tormented mankind from the beginning! That Devil who has placed sin, sickness and sorrow on us! That Devil who has even preachers afraid of him! Let us walk up to that Devil and let us mention the Name of Jesus! And the Devil himself, will bow to that Name!

Now let us come back to earth. We have seen that every knee in Heaven will bow to the Name of Jesus! We have seen that every knee in Hell will bow to the Name of Jesus! Now I want you to know that every knee on earth will bow to the Name of Jesus! Every sickness, every sin, every sorrow, every demon, every power of any kind, will bow to the Name of Jesus! And you have a right to use That Name!

Right now you can decree a thing in the Name of Jesus! You can speak in the Name of Jesus! You can announce and declare in the Name of Jesus! You have the right to do it! You have the authority to do it! You have His permission to do it! Declare your healing in the Name of Jesus! Declare your deliverance in the Name of Jesus! Then believe it, confess it and act on it!

CHAPTER 5

THE WILL OF GOD

Even after understanding all that has been said so far, the average person is still tormented by doubt. Satan still tries to talk us out of what the Bible plainly teaches is ours. One other thing that the Devil uses to make us doubt is whether or not, it is God's will to give us what we are asking for.

How do we know that it is God's Will to heal us? How do we know it is His will to give us what we are asking for? How can I know God's Will? Is it God's will to heal everyone? Is it God's will to save everyone? Is it God's Will to prosper everyone? Is it God's Will that some should be blessed and others should suffer? How can we know?

These are legitimate questions and there are answers! The Bible has the Answer! Let us talk about healing for a moment. Is it God's will to heal everyone? As far as I am concerned, this question was answered by Jesus Himself.

NO RESPECTER OF PERSONS

In the eighth chapter of Matthew, when he was coming down from the Mount of Transfiguration, He was met by a leper. The man said to Him, "Lord, if thou wilt, thou canst make me whole." Jesus answered, "I will. Be thou made whole." And immediately the man's leprosy was healed! Now put this in modern language. The man said, "Lord. if you are willing, you can make me whole." Jesus said, "I am willing. Be thou made whole."

Now to me, this answers the question! One may say that Jesus was talking to that Leper, but the Scripture tells us that God is no respecter of persons! If He was willing to heal one Leper, He is willing to heal another Leper. If He was willing to heal one blind man, He is willing to heal another blind man! If He was willing to heal one cripple man, He is willing to heal another cripple man! You see, He cannot be a respecter of people!

CHURCH DOCTRINE

Most Full Gospel Churches that I know, have a Statement of Faith, much like My own Denomination. The Statement says, "We believe Divine Healing is provided for all in the Atonement." Now look at this statement for a moment. If God has provided Divine Healing for all in the Atonement, then it is God's Will for all to be healed! He would not have provided, in the Atonement, something that He was not willing for us to have! In other words, if God is not willing to heal me, then He has not provided healing for me. He has not provided something that is against His Will. So if it is not His will to heal me, then my church will have to change it's Statement of Faith! We would have to say, "We believe Divine Healing is provided for all, (Except Franklin Hunt) in the Atonement. Thank God, our forefathers in the Church, knew what the Bible teaches! The Statement is right, because it is based on the Word of God! God has already provided healing for us! We must believe it, Confess it and act on it!

THE LORD'S PRAYER

If you need more convincing, look at the Lord's Prayer. The disciples came to Jesus and asked Him to teach them to pray. Jesus said, "When you pray, say, 'Our Father, Who art in Heaven, Hallowed be Thy Name. Thy Kingdom come. Thy will be done on earth as it is in Heaven." (Lk. 11:1-4)

Now look at this prayer! We have repeated it many times, but do you understand what it is saying? It is telling us, that whatever the Father's Will is, it is being done in Heaven! Right now, God's Will is being done in Heaven!

Now let us in our imagination, ascend to Heaven. Behold all the beauty and splendor there. Now tell me what you see! Do you see that hospital on the hill, for the many sick people there? Do you see a blind man, with a cane, tapping his way down the Golden street? Do you see a crippled man sitting there in a wheelchair? Of course not! You do not see one sick or disabled person in Heaven! Why?

Let us ask someone. Let us ask Gabriel.

"Gabriel, I notice that there are no sick people in heaven."

"You are right. There are no sick people here."

"But why are there no sick people here?"

"Because the Father's Will is being done here."

"Gabriel, do you mean that it is God's Will for every person in Heaven to be well?"

"Yes, it is God's Will that everyone here be well."

"But is it not God's will that some suffer, maybe for things they have done in the past?"

"No. Jesus paid for their past. They are redeemed, well and happy."

"Thank you Gabriel. I must go back to earth and tell the good news! If it is God's Will for everyone in Heaven to be well, it is God's Will for everyone in Earth to be well!"

You see, He taught us to pray, that God's Will will be done on earth as it is being done in Heaven! Do not let anything make you doubt that it is God's Will to heal you, or to give you any other good thing that He has promised!

DOCTORS AND MEDICINE

If it is not God's will to heal you, then it is wrong to seek treatment! It amazes me that many modern preachers will tell you it is not God's will to heal, and then recommend a Doctor for you to see!

Now think for a minute. If you have a tumor and it is not God's Will to Heal you, then it is God's will for you to keep the tumor! You see, it is either His Will for you to keep it or it is His Will for you to be rid of it (Healed)! So if it is not His Will to heal you, then He wants you to keep it! Now if is His will for you to have this tumor, are you going to the Surgeon and have him cut God's Will out of you? You may think I am being silly, but this is simple logic!

If you are sick and it is not God's will to heal you, then it is His Will for you to be sick. Thus if you seek treatment, you are seeking to go against God's Will! Can you understand this simple logic. It is either God's Will to heal you or it is His Will for you to be sick!

Now Satan may give you many reasons as to why God wants you sick. None of them are true. In a later chapter in this book, I will answer these 'reasons' that Satan uses to try to make you doubt your deliverance. As for now, I want you to know it is not wrong to seek healing, from God or from Doctors and Medicine. They are all designed to make me well.

The fact is, God has put a process of healing in you and me. This is another proof that God wants to heal us. You see, the only reason that Medical science can exist at all, is because there is a healing process in our body.

For example, if you should cut your finger, which many of us do, often in our day to day lives, You would bleed to death, if there was not a healing process in you! You could go to the Doctor and he could stitch the cut and bandage it, but that would not heal it! What actually happens is that the moment you cut your finger, White corpuscles rush to the surface to fight off infection. If this did not happen, you would die from a half inch cut. Then the blood begins to coagulate to stop the bleeding. Then the skin and flesh immediately begin to procreate new cells to grow the flesh back together. Now no medicine or treatment causes these things to happen. They happen because God has placed a healing process in you!

I could write an entire book on this healing process! It works with any and everything that comes against your health! If you catch a cold, you get a million different germs in your respiratory system. You know that there is no cure for the common cold, except to get rest, drink liquids and wait eight to ten days. The reason there is no cure, is because there are so many different germs involved. But you have in you, a system that takes each one of these germs, analyzes it and then builds an antibody to destroy it! It takes eight to ten days, because there are so many different germs to analyze and destroy. This wonderful system was created in you, by God! Can you doubt any more, that it is God's Will to heal you? He built healing in you! When you are sick, seek a good doctor and treatment and seek a good Saint to pray for you! They are all trying to get you well! There is no conflict between medicine and miracles! Neither the pills of one nor the prayers of the other are your source of your healing. All healing comes from God!

Medicine only works, because God has placed within us, a system, that interacts with the Medicine! For example, the only reason an aspirin relieves pain, is because there is a system within us that reacts to the ingredients in aspirin. If this system was not there, we would get no more reaction from an aspirin than we do from a jelly bean! God wants us well so much that He places this wonderful healing system within us! Many people hear all of this and still have doubts. Their question is, "If God wants to heal everyone, then why are people still sick?"

Let me ask another question that will help answer this one. If God wants to save everyone, why are people still lost? You see, the two questions are the same. God provided both salvation and healing in the Atonement. We know that it is God's will to save everyone. His Word says, "It is not God's will that any should perish, but that all should come to repentance." So we know it is God's will to save everyone! Why are so many still lost? Here is why.

Some are lost because they have never heard the message of salvation. God has chosen preaching of the Word, to save the lost. (1 Cor. 1:21) How can they believe if they have not heard? That is why it is so important to get the Gospel to everyone! Then some have heard but have not understood.

They are still lost. They must understand that salvation is for them also. Many still believe that some people are destined to be saved and some are destined to be lost. They need to understand that God wants to save everyone! Then some are lost, because they have heard and understood, but have not believed. Many people who have heard and understood the Gospel, still refuse to believe. They refuse to accept their own salvation. They may let false doctrine, or creed or other religious concepts keep them from accepting what Christ has done for them. You see, even though it is God's will to save everyone, there are still many millions lost, because of the reasons given above. But everyone who has heard, understood, believed and accepted Christ, is saved!

The same thing applies to healing. It is God's will to heal! But some have never heard the message of healing. How can they be healed if they have never heard?

Some have heard but have not understood. They need to understand that their own personal healing was provided in the Atonement! They need to understand that healing is for them!

Then some have heard and understood, but have not believed! Many have heard the message of healing, but still refuse to believe it. They let false doctrine or creed or other religious concepts keep them from believing and receiving their healing! Yet the proof is right before their eyes! There are millions of people who have heard, understood, believed and received their healing!

They are healed today! You can be one of these! You have read this far in this book! You now understand that God has provided healing for you! Now believe it and accept your healing! It is yours!

58

LOOKING AT THE WILL OF GOD

Let us take one more look at the proof of God's Will. We have God's Will already written and given to us! We can read it for ourselves!

Your Bible is divided into two Testaments. The Old Testament and the New Testament. Did you know that a testament and a will are one and the same thing? If you go to hear someone's will read, it will state, 'The last will and testament of John Doe.' This comes from a tradition that goes back to the days in old England, when everything was read in English and in French. So Will and testament are simply French and English words which mean the same thing. Your Bible could be called The Old Will and The New Will. It would mean the same thing as Old Testament and New Testament.

Now consider this. The Old Testament is the Will of God The Father. It was Willed to a certain group of people, Abraham's Seed, the Israelites. It was willed on the basis that they keep God's Law. Example, "If you will keep my statutes and my commandments, then I will allow none of these diseases to come upon you." (Ex. 15:26) Every promise in the Old Will, of healing or blessing or prosperity, was based on keeping the Law. But every person who ever lived, broke the Law! All except one! The Israelites broke the Law and lost their inheritance! Not one person was ever justified by keeping the Law! (Rom. 3:20) All have sinned and come short of the Glory of God. (Rom. 3:23) All but one!

You see, Jesus had to be born of the Jews, to put Him in line for the inheritance! He was a Jew and He never sinned! He fulfilled the Law to the Letter!

Now when a will is made, it is of no force, until the person who makes the will, dies. If some friend or kinsperson put your name in their will and willed you a thousand dollars, you could not touch that thousand dollars until that person died. Once they die, the money is yours! It is not yours because you have earned it, or deserve it! It is yours because they willed it to you! A testament or will is of force, after men are dead.

Now look at the Old Will. It was the last will and testament of God the Father. But God could not die! So He allowed part of His Creation to die. He had the priests of old, to slay lambs, goats and bulls, to shed blood to seal His Will. The Bible teaches all of this in the book of Hebrews! Look at Hebrews 9:16-20:

'For where a testament is, there must also of necessity be the death of the testator. For a testament is of force after men are dead. Otherwise it is of no strength at all, while the testator liveth. Whereupon neither the first testament was dedicated without blood. For when Moses had spoken every precept to all the people, according to the law, he took the blood of calves and of goats with water, and scarlet wool, and hyssop, and sprinkled both the book and all the people, Saying, This is the Blood of the Testament which God hath enjoined unto you!

Do you see that the Old Testament was the last will and testament of God and that God sealed this testament with the Blood of animals, because God could not die!

Now understand that Jesus totally fulfilled the Law! He inherited every promise in the Old Testament! He could say, "All Power in Heaven and in earth is given unto me." (Mt. 28:18) He had inherited everything that the Father had willed to Him! Then on the night of the Last Supper, Jesus took the cup and passed it to His Disciples, saying, "Drink ye all of it, for this is My Blood of the New Testament." (Mt. 26:27-28)

At the time Jesus said this, the New Testament had not been written. But Jesus is saying to His Disciples, "I am going to leave a Will and I am going to seal it with my own Blood." The New Testament is the last Will and Testament of Jesus! Now look at Heb. 9:15:

'And for this cause, He is the mediator of the New Testament. That by means of death for the redemption of the transgressions that were under the first testament, they which are called, might receive the Promise of eternal inheritance.'

This is wonderful! Jesus has left a last will and testament! Now the question is, 'Who did He leave it to?' Jesus did not leave His will to those who keep the Law! That was the Old Will. It is sad that many in Christian circles today, still try to put the Law on born again Christians. They still try to put us back into the Old Testament, which has been fulfilled and replaced with a New Testament! Jesus did not leave His will to those who keep the Sabbath or any other Holy day. He did not leave His will to those who perform Rites or Ceremonies! He did not leave His will to those who make sacrifices or live ultra holy lives! Who did He will His Blessings to? Over three hundred times in His Will it is told that it is to those who believe! It is willed to those who accept Him by Faith and live by Faith! If you can believe, All things are possible to him that believeth! (Mk. 9:23)

This is almost too wonderful to comprehend! Everything in the New Testament is willed to you and me, if we will simply believe! Sadly, we let so many doubts talk us out of our inheritance! We need to stand up for what is legally ours. Satan is always trying to cause us to doubt.

Suppose a relative were to die and leave you a small piece of land in his will. Then suppose crooked kinsfolk and their lawyers tried to take it away from you. What would you do? You would go to court and fight for what is legally yours! On the Stand, the lawyers might ask you, did you earn it. You would say, "No, but it is still mine."

They may ask if you think you deserve it. You would answer, "No, but it is still mine."

They may then ask, why you think it is yours if you did not earn it nor deserve it. You would answer, "It is mine, because it was willed to me."

You see, Satan tries to drag us into the court of the Law. He tries to tell us that we have not been good enough nor do we deserve the Blessings of Christ. We need to remind Satan that we realize that we are not good enough nor holy enough to deserve anything God has. But we are going to have it, because He willed it to us! It is ours! He wants us to have it! He willed it to us and He died to seal His Will!

Many men have died and left a will. Many times, crooked people have taken inheritances away from those to whom it was willed. But consider this! Jesus is the only man who ever died to seal His will and then rose from the dead to become the executor of His own will! What does that mean? It means that when you stand up in Faith and claim what Jesus has left you, Jesus, Himself, will stand in court with you! He is the Author and He is the Finisher of the whole matter! (Heb. 12:2) Satan will have to retreat!

The New Testament is the last will and testament of Jesus! It is willed to believers. If your name is in the Lamb's Book of Life, then your name is in the Will!

Now what does this mean to me as a preacher? It means I can go to the vilest sinner and tell him that, no matter what he has done, Jesus will save him! How can I tell everyone that? Because I read in the Will, "Him that cometh unto me, I will in no wise cast out." (Jn. 6:37) Jesus will not turn anyone away! I can go to any believer and tell him that Jesus will baptize him with The Holy Spirit! How can I tell everyone that Jesus wants to baptize them with The Holy Spirit? Because I read in the will, "The Promise is unto you and to your children and to all them that are far off, even as many as the Lord, our God shall call." (Acts 2:39)

Likewise, I can go to the sick and say, "God will heal you!" How can I tell everyone that God will heal them? Because I read in the Will, "Is any among you sick? Let him call for the elders of the church and let them pray over him, anointing him with oil. And the prayer of faith shall save the sick and the Lord shall raise him up." (Jas. 5:14-15)

Look at what it says. It does not say if any of the chosen few are sick, the Lord will raise them up. It says, "any among you." Anybody among you will be raised up! Not somebody, but anybody! I love this Scripture! I may never qualify to be a "Somebody" But even I am an "anybody"!

I have heard people preach that the Lord will not heal sinners. Is it not amazing that people will say this, but when some of their lost loved ones get sick, they will request prayer for them. This scripture teaches that God will heal anybody, who has faith! Look at what it says: "The prayer of faith shall save the sick and the Lord shall raise him up. And if he hath committed any sins, they shall be forgiven him." How loving and wonderful is our God. He wants to save everybody! He wants to Fill everybody! He wants to heal everybody!

Now go to the Will. Find a promise for whatever you need. Now claim that promise as your inheritance!

Do you have a financial need? Here is what is willed to you! "My God shall supply all your need, according to His riches in Glory, by Christ Jesus." (Phil. 4:19)

Do you need to be filled with The Spirit? Here is what is willed to you: "Receive ye the Holy Spirit. (in. 20:22)"

Do you need better health? Here is what is willed to you: "Beloved, I would, above all things, that thou wouldest prosper and be in health, even as thy soul prospereth." (3 Jn. v 2) I could go on and on! Every promise in the Will is mine! Not because I am good or deserving. It is mine, because Jesus willed it to me!

Now let us go back to the nineth chapter of Hebrews and the thirteenth verse: "For if the blood of bulls and goats and the ashes of an heifer, sprinkling the unclean, sanctifieth to the purifying of the flesh: How much more shall the Blood of Christ, who through the Eternal Spirit offered Himself without spot to God, purge your conscience from dead works to the Living God."

Look at this! If we can have confidence in the Old Testament, which was sealed with the Blood of animals, How much more confidence can we have in the New Testament, which was sealed with the actual Blood of Christ?

Rise up in faith and boldness now and claim your inheritance! There is a story of a young lady in Russia, some years ago, when the church had to operate under ground, who was on her way to church. She was stopped by the KGB and asked where she was going. She knew that she could not expose the church to great danger, but neither could she tell a lie. The Lord put words in her mouth! She answered, "I am on my way to my Father's House. My elder Brother has died and I am going to see what He left me in His will."

That is exactly why we go to church! Our Elder Brother, Jesus, has died and we go to see what He left us in His Will! And you know what I have found out? He left it all to me! Everything in that Will is mine! He willed it to me!

CHAPTER 6

WHY ARE PEOPLE SICK

Jesus said, "The thief cometh not but for to steal and to kill and to destroy. I am come that you might have life and that you might have it more abundantly." (Jn. 10:10) So why are people sick?

Many good, God loving, Christian people have asked this question. Their thinking is, "I love God. I try to serve Him. So why am I sick? Why has God allowed this to happen to me? Why are my children sick? What have I done?"

There are many Ministers and theologians who have many theories to answer these questions. They teach that people are sick because they are being punished for something they or someone else has done. They teach that people are sick because God wants to teach them a lesson or try them out, to see if they will remain faithful. Some teach that people are sick, so that God can get glory out of their sickness. It amazes me, how many ideas people can come up with, that are not taught in the Word of God. I want to discuss some of these theories and ideas and show you the real reason that people are sick and how they can be healed. I want to tear down some of these ideas, so that you can have faith for the miracle you need!

SICKNESS IS NOT
GOD'S PUNISHMENT FOR SIN!

The first thing I want to tell you, is that sickness is not God punishing you for sin! I think of all the theories I hear, I dislike this one the most. I am feeling bad enough, when I am sick, without someone telling me that I have sinned and thus God is punishing me for it. This is what Job's "comforters" tried to tell him. They tried to convince him that he had sinned and that God was punishing him for it. But Job had a fixed faith! He said, "Let me tell you something. I know that my Redeemer lives. And though He slay me, I will trust Him. And though the skin worms destroy this body, yet in my flesh, I shall see God. I shall see Him for myself and not another!" (Jb. 19:25-27) Job was not being punished for sin!

The Disciples had this same misconception at one time. They found a man who had been born blind. They asked Jesus, "Master, who did sin, this man, or his parents, that this man was born blind?" Now it is evident that the man had not sinned, because he was born blind. He could not have sinned before he was born. But what about his parents? Did they sin, before the man was born and cause their child to be born blind? "Jesus answered, Neither hath this man sinned nor his parents. But that the works of God should be made manifest in him." (Jn. 19:1-3) The question is answered here! This sickness was not a punishment for sin!

People who believe that God punishes sin, with sickness, have a misunderstanding of sin and salvation. Sin is punished, but it is dealt with in only one way. "The wages of sin is death." (Rom. 6:23) The only way that sin can be dealt with is through death! You can never pay for sin! You can never pay for even one sin. That is why Hell is eternal.

There are some who believe that if you suffer enough in this life, you will automatically go to heaven. They teach that you are suffering for your sins and when you have paid for them, you will make it to Heaven. They also teach that if you have not suffered enough here, you will suffer after death, until your sins have been paid for. They even go as far as to teach, that after you are dead, your loved ones can help pay for your sins, by giving money or suffering in your place. None of this is taught in Scripture.

We have all sinned. "All have sinned and come short of the Glory of God." (Rom. 3:23) Now think, if cancer was the punishment for sin, we would all have cancer! If arthritis was the punishment for sin, we would all have arthritis. There is only one penalty for sin and that is death! Not just the death of the body, but separation from God, after death. That is why, Jesus died! Since I have sinned, I can never pay for my own sin. No matter what I do. No matter how much I suffer. No matter how much good I try to do. Sin can only be paid for by separation from God and it can never be fully paid for! Hell is eternal. A million years in Hell, still will not pay for even one of my sins! I have sinned and I am guilty. The wages of sin is death and can never be paid for.

Are we all, then, lost forever? No! Since I cannot pay for my own sins, I needed someone who never committed any sin, to be willing to die in my place! And that is what Jesus did! He did not die for His own sin. He never committed any sin. He died for our sins!

That is why, when He hung on the Cross, He cried, "My God, My God, why hast Thou forsaken me?" He had to be separated from God, because of our sins! God laid the punishment of all of our sins, on Him! Jesus was punished for my sins!

Now since God has punished Jesus for my sins, He cannot justly punish me again for my sins. If I will accept what Jesus has done for me, then I can go free!

When a person repents of their sins, God blots them out. He remembers them no more! Now how can He punish you for something He does not even remember! Thank God, when we come to Christ, our sins are gone, never to be remembered again!

Sin is dealt with, either at Calvary or at The Judgment. Your sins have either already been dealt with at Calvary or they will face you at the Judgment. I thank God, mine have already been dealt with! Mine are gone and I will never be punished for them nor reminded of them!

SICKNESS CAN BE A RESULT OF SIN.

While Sickness in not God's punishment for sin, sickness can be a result of sin. A person can drink so much alcohol that he gets cirrhosis of the liver. He may think that God is punishing him for drinking, but the truth is, God had nothing to do with it! The alcohol caused the sickness! A person may smoke until he gets lung cancer. He may blame God for putting the lung cancer on him for smoking. But, again, God had nothing to do with it. The smoking caused the cancer!

We can live all kinds of lifestyles that bring diseases on our bodies. But it is us doing it! It is not God punishing us for our stupidity! If we drive careless and have a wreck and injure someone, it is not God doing it! We need to remember that Satan wants to kill us. We should not live any lifestyle that would give Satan a chance to kill us!

Satan brought sickness into the world, at the fall of Adam and Eve. He brought all of his destructive forces, to try to destroy mankind. But, thank God, Jesus came to redeem us from the power of the Devil and give back, everything that Satan tried to take away! Do not let anyone tell you that God is punishing you, by making you sick! God loves you! He wants to save you, heal you, deliver you and bless you!

SICKNESS IS NOT A TRIAL FROM GOD

Another theory that I want to deal with is the one that says, God has sent sickness to try you. Some believe that God is putting them through some kind of trial and when He has finished trying them, He will heal them. I simply cannot accept such teaching. Why would God need to try me?

God knows me! He knows the number of hairs on my head! He knows my weaknesses and my strengths! He knows my going out and my coming in! He knows my lying down and my rising up! He knows exactly how much I can bear! He said He would not allow me to be tempted above what I am able to bear. In other words, He will not even allow Satan to tempt me, beyond what I am capable of handling. If He did not know what I can bear, how would He know when to stop the Devil?

The Bible tells us that if we earthly fathers know how to give good things to our children, how much more does our Heavenly Father know how to give good things to His children. (Mt. 7:11) What kind of father would I be, if I took a red hot fire coal and put it on my child and watched him scream in pain and said, "Son I just want to see if you trust me?" I would be arrested and locked up! Only a demented father would do such a thing! Yet people believe that our Father, God, does such things! What kind of Father would God be, if He put an eating cancer on one of His children and said, "I just want to see if you trust me"? This is not the kind of Father we have! My Father is not trying to kill me, He is trying to heal me!

This was shown to me, when my first child was born. Camy was born with a condition that caused her great pain. Sometimes she would cry for days. We took her to several doctors. She was put on several medications, but nothing seemed to help. One day she had cried so much, it had greatly upset my wife. She said, "I am going somewhere to find help for my child." She left to go talk to another doctor. I held my child in my arms. We had prayed for her many times. I looked up and said, "God, I love this child so much that if I could take this pain and put it in my own body, I would do so." The Lord spoke to me! He said, "Franklin, I love that child more than you do. I have already taken her pains and put them in my Son's Body." I was shocked! I immediately rebuked Satan. I said "Devil, Jesus has borne this sickness and you have no right to torment my child. She is healed!" My child stopped crying! When my wife returned I told her what had happened. My daughter was never bothered with that pain again. Today she is married and has two children of her own!

People quote scripture to back up their thinking. They say, "Whom the Lord loveth He also chaseneth." That is true. The Lord corrects His Children. I correct my children, but I do not beat them so bad that they have to go to the hospital! That is abuse! There are laws against abuse! My Heavenly Father gently and lovingly corrects me and guides me, but He does not abuse me. I wonder sometimes if we will ever really embrace the real Love of God. It is almost as if we are afraid to accept how much God really loves us! His Love is unconditional! We are afraid to say that. We feel that we must teach that God is harsh and brutal, in order to force people to live right. We try to scare people into serving God. But God wants us to serve Him, because we love Him! Those who preach a "God is going to get you for that" type of Gospel, forget that it is the Goodness of God that draws men to repentance!

God is not trying you out with some dreaded sickness or disease. He loves you. He wants you to have life! He wants you to be prosperous and in good health, just as much as He wants your soul saved!

SICKNESS IS NOT FOR GOD'S GLORY

Another theory I want to dispel is the idea that sickness is for God's Glory. Many people have been taught that they are sick for the purpose of glorifying God. This notion contradicts everything that Jesus did! If sickness was going to glorify God, then Jesus would have gone around, putting sickness on people. Instead, the Bible says that, "God anointed Jesus of Nazareth with the Holy Ghost and with power, who went about, doing good and healing all who were oppressed of the Devil, for God was with Him." (Acts 10:38)

Jesus went around healing people, not making them sick! And he said that He came to Glorify the Father.

Now think for a moment: If sickness is going to glorify God, then we should have prayer lines, in which we pray for people to have some sickness placed on them, that they might glorify God in a greater way! Yet, instead, we have prayer lines, in which we pray for people to be healed! Which makes more sense? If sickness is glorifying God, we should not pray for healing. Instead, we should pray to remain sick, so that our Father can be glorified!

Many people think that the scripture, which I have already referred to, about the man born blind, teaches that sickness glorifies God. But that is not what it says! The Disciples asked, who had sinned that this man was born blind. Jesus said no one had sinned to cause this, but that the Works of God might be manifested in Him. Now what did Jesus do? He healed the man! The Work of God was manifested in his healing, not in his sickness! Did anyone glorify God for him while he was sick? Of course not! But when He was healed, people glorified God. It was his healing that glorified God, not his sickness! When we see someone sick today, do we begin to glorify God for it? We do not! We begin to pray for the sick and have compassion on him. But when we see him healed, we glorify God! Do you see the difference?

People will say that they want to glorify God, with their whole being. So if your cancer or diabetes is glorifying God, then you should not pray or take treatment for it. You should want to keep it, in order to glorify God.

We have better sense than this. Do you get glory out of your children being sick? Does it lift you up in spirit to watch your child suffer in pain? Of course not! Neither does God get glory out of watching His children suffer!

If a plague of sickness should hit and many of God's people have to stay out of work and stay out of church and not be able to tithe or give to God, would this glorify Him? The church doors would have to close. World Missions would have to cease. The Gospel could not go forward! The lost would not be reached. Would God get glory out of this?

No, my friend. God wants you to be able to work and earn money and support your family and tithe and give to help the Gospel go forward! This is what glorifies God!

Now I realize that some people have gotten sick and gone to a hospital and while they were there, they witnessed to someone. But the sickness was not for God's glory. God took advantage of the situation and had that person witness to someone while they were there. But would it not have been better to visit the Hospital and witness to the sick, while you were well? It is a shame, if we have to get sick enough to go to the hospital, before we will go there and witness and pray for the sick. Please note that not one time, did Jesus ever find a·healthy person and say, "1 am going to put a sickness on you, so that you may glorify my Father." Even when the Disciples wanted to call fire down from Heaven and burn their enemies, Jesus said, "You know not what spirit you are of. I did not come to kill men, but to save them alive." (Lk. 9:54-56)

You see! He wants me alive! He wants me well! He provided healing for me in the Atonement! I go about, every day, praising God for my good health! God wants you well so that you can glorify Him! Throughout the Bible, when people saw God heal others, they were amazed and glorified God!

74

SICKNESS IS OF THE DEVIL

So what have we learned so far?

One, Sickness is not God's punishment for sin!

Two, Sickness is not a trial from God!

Three, Sickness is not for God's Glory!

So what is sickness?

Where does it come from?

Why are people sick?

The answer is simple! Sickness is of the Devil! People have a hard time understanding that. I was a Christian for sixteen years, before I found out that sickness is of the Devil. I was a Spirit filled Christian. I was in a Spirit filled church. I had been miraculously healed, myself! Yet no one had taught me that sickness was of the Devil! I had heard all the theories that I have just addressed. I had been taught that sometimes sickness was this and sometimes it was that and sometimes we could never know why the sickness was on us. I had been taught that sometimes the Devil put it on us and sometimes God put it on us and sometimes, we put it on ourselves! No wonder the sick are confused!

Then one day, I read a sermon, wherein a Minister said that sickness was of the Devil. I did not like it. I disagreed with the man. I went and opened my Bible and began to read to prove that the Minister was wrong! Some people who read this book will probably try to do the same thing. But the more I read, the more I became convinced that the Bible plainly teaches that sickness if of the Devil.

I read where the Bible says, "God anointed Jesus of Nazareth, with the Holy Ghost and with power, who went about doing good and healing all who were oppressed of the

Devil" (Acts 10:38). There it is! Satan made people sick. Jesus healed them I looked at the book of Job. I had always thought that God had afflicted Job. Yet I read that, "Satan went forward and smote Job from the crown of his head to the soles of his feet with boils." (Jb. 2:7)

It was Satan who smote Job!

Then I took a closer look at the Ministry of Jesus. When a blind man came for healing, Jesus rebuked a blind spirit. When a deaf man came to be healed, Jesus rebuked a deaf spirit. When a boy who had seizures was brought for healing, Jesus rebuked a spirit. When a little lady came to Him, bowed over and paralyzed, the people said that He should not heal on the Sabbath. Jesus, said, "Doth not each one of you, on the Sabbath, loose his ox or ass from the stall and lead him away to watering? And ought not this woman, being a daughter of Abraham, whom Satan hath bound, lo these eighteen years, be loosed from this bond on the Sabbath day?" (Luke 13:15-16) Jesus said that Satan had bound her!

Then I began to reason, If God makes people sick and then Jesus heals them, then Jesus is working contrary to the Father. But Jesus said, "I work the works of Him that sent me." (John 9:4) So if God sometimes put sickness on people, then Jesus would have met some people and said to them, "I cannot heal you, because my Father has put that on you." But Jesus knew that His Father had not done any such thing. He knew that His Father loved people, and had sent Him to heal them! It was love that sent Jesus down here to redeem people from the power of the Devil!

The Scripture plainly says, "For this purpose, the Son of God was manifested, that He might destroy the works of the

Devil." (1 John, 3:8) Do you see it? When Jesus healed the lame or the blind or the deaf, whose works was He destroying? If these were God's works, then Jesus and God were at odds with one another. But Jesus was destroying the works of the Devil!

Sickness is of the Devil! It is the Devil that causes sickness! It is Satan who puts lameness, blindness, diabetes, cancer and heart trouble on people! It is Jesus who heals them! The very proof that Jesus was the Son of God, was the type of works that He did. When John the Baptist sent and asked, "are you the Son of God or do we look for another?" Jesus said "Go and shew John again those things which ye do hear and see. The blind receive their sight, and the lame walk, the lepers are cleaned, and the deaf hear, the dead are raised up, and the poor have the Gospel preached to them." (Matt. 10:3-5) Now if these things had been of the Devil, John would have known it right away. But when John heard of the works, He knew that this was Christ! John rested in peace. You see, John had come to announce the coming of Christ. When he knew that Christ had come, he knew that his work was over. Soon after this, he went home to Heaven.

Again, remember, The Thief (the Devil) cometh not, but for to steal, and to kill, and to destroy... (John 10:10) Jesus said the Devil is come to steal your health, steal your wealth, steal your happiness, and to kill you and to destroy everything that you have. But, then Jesus said, "I am come that they might have life, and that they might have it more abundantly." Do you hear what I am telling you?

Satan first tries to attack your mind. He cannot touch your spirit, so he has two other avenues. He tries to attack your mind and body. You know what it is to have Satan attack your mind. He tries to fill you with doubt, worry, fear, He will tell you every kind of lie. He will give you every kind of temptation, throw everything in your path, try to discourage you, try to make you and your mate fight, try to destroy your marriage, and anything else he can do to destroy you. He does not care how he does it. It does not matter with him, if you are on nerve pills or drugs or alcohol. It does not matter with him, if you have a nervous breakdown or lose your mind. He just wants to destroy you.

If he cannot destroy your mind, he will go to work on your body. He will put every kind of pain, sickness, symptom or feeling on your body to get you to doubt, fear, ache, hurt, and suffer. He does not care how much you hurt. He does not care how much you spend on doctors and treatment. He does not care how much you suffer. He only wants to destroy you.

I have seen the Devil jump pains around on people. You get rid of one pain and another starts in another part of the body. He will jump cancer around on a person. The Devil will tell you, "Well, you got healed of that one, but this is a different one." Let me tell you something. God loves you! He is not trying to kill you or destroy you. He is trying to give you life! He is trying to give you abundant life! Satan wants to make you believe a lie!

He wants to make you believe that God is punishing you for something, or that He is trying you out for some reason, or that He is making you suffer, so that He can get some kind of Glory out of it. This is all a lie! My sins are forgiven through faith in Christ. Jesus was punished for my sins and I do not have to be punished for them. God does not have to try me out, because He already knows me. He knows what I can and cannot bear. God does not get Glory out of seeing his children suffer, any more than we get glory out of the suffering of our own children. Praise God, He loves me and wants to give me life!

Right now, you can raise your hands and praise Him! You can shout the victory! You can have full confidence that God wants only good things for you! You can receive your healing! You can claim it, even before it is manifested! You can stand on His Word and declare that you are healed by the Stripes of Jesus! His Word is sure and will not change! His promise is to you, just as much as it is to anyone in the world! If God will do it for anyone else, He will do it for you! If He is not willing to heal you, then He is not willing to heal anybody in the world! If His promises are for anybody, then they are for you

CHAPTER 7

THE PURPOSE OF FAITH

With all that has been said so far, there still will be many people who will fail to receive by faith, because they do not know the real purpose of faith. Many people believe that if they just have enough faith, they will never be sick, they will never have a need, they will never face a problem of any kind. This way of thinking will surely cause you to fail in your believing. You must understand the purpose of faith.

FAITH OR FOOLISHNESS

Because people do not know the real purpose of faith, they get entrapped in doing some very foolish things. I have seen people who would not buy health or life insurance, because they thought they would never get sick and I guess they thought they would never die. But the Scripture is very specific in stating that it is appointed unto men to die. Everyone of the men and women of God in the Bible, died. To think that you can have enough faith to keep you alive forever, on this earth, is to live in foolishness rather than faith!

Sickness, disease, troubles and sorrows are all weapons from Satan, to try to destroy us or destroy our faith. If we think that faith will keep us from ever facing any of these things, we deceive ourselves. We are in a war. We wrestle with the demons and weapons of Satan.

I have known people who would not take an immunity shot or take medicine or go to a doctor, thinking they were walking in faith. As much as I respect their courage, I have to sound an alarm here. This is a misunderstanding of faith! Doctors and medicine do not conflict with miracles and faith! In fact, they all work together! You see, medicine would not work, if God had not put a system in your body, designed to interact with the medicine! Surgery would not work, if God had not put a system in your body, to heal the wound of surgery and restore your body back to normal. When you understand this, you realize that all healing comes from God! Whether you take medicine, therapy, surgery, prayer or worship, all healing comes from God! It is God who put a system of healing in our bodies! It is God who put vitamins, minerals, proteins and medicines in this world! It is God who gives knowledge to doctors and researchers! You see, researchers do not create, they discover! They discover the wonderful things that God has put here for our benefit! Every good and perfect gift comes from our God!

Many people say that they are trusting God with their health, but you must remember, God is trusting you with your health! No matter how much faith, you have, if you continue to abuse your body, with things that are dangerous or unclean for your body, you will continue to destroy your health.

I believe that healing is up to God, but health is up to me! God will not go against my will. If I want to continue putting things into my body that will destroy it, then God will let me do so. He loves me and wants to save and heal me! He has done everything that He could do to keep me in peace and health and safety. But He has placed a responsibility on me to do my part. I do not believe God will do for me, what I am capable of doing for myself!

For example, I believe God wants me to write this book. I believe He gives me inspiration and revelation to write it. But I do not believe He is going to sit down and type it out for me. Why? Because I am capable of doing it myself! He has given me the strength, the ability and the knowledge, but He will not do it for me!

Therefore, God expects me to do all that I can to keep my body in good health and strength. He expects me to eat right, to the best of my knowledge. He expects me to exercise right. He expects me to keep unclean things out of my body. He expects me to Glorify Him with my body, soul and spirit!

Therefore, it is right for me to carry insurance on myself, for a defense against the attacks of Satan and for the security of my family. He expects me to do whatever I can to keep myself immune to the diseases of this world. He expects me to keep myself and my family safe, to the best of my ability. When I have done all that I can, then my faith in God will do the rest!

WHAT FAITH IS DESIGNED FOR

We must understand that faith was never designed to keep us from a storm. Faith was never designed to keep us from a trial. Faith was never designed to keep us from persecution. Faith was never designed to keep us from suffering. FAITH IS DESIGNED TO BRING US THROUGH THESE THINGS! Notice the word 'through'.

82

Faith did not keep Daniel out of the lions den. Faith brought him through it! Faith did not keep the Hebrew boys out of the fiery furnace. Faith brought them through it! Faith did not keep Paul out of a storm. Faith brought him through it! All of the people of faith in the Bible, went through persecution, tribulation, pain, beatings, imprisonments and every other kind of torture. But they were people of great faith! It was their faith that brought them through everything that Satan could bring against them!

Look at some awesome words in the eleventh chapter of Hebrews: The first thirty one verses tell of the things done by faith, by Abel, Enoch, Noah, Abraham, Sarah, Isaac, Jacob, Joseph, Moses and Rahab,the harlot. Then the thirty second verse names Gedeon, Barak, Sampson, Japhthae, David, Samuel and the prophets. The thirty third verse says through faith these people subdued kingdoms, wrought righteousness, obtained promises, stopped the mouths of lions, quenched the violence of fire, escaped the edge of the sword, were made strong in weakness, waxed valiant in fight, turned to flight the armies of enemies and saw the dead raised! Then the thirty sixth verse begins to tell that others with the same faith, had trials of cruel mockings and scourgings and of bonds and imprisonment. Some were stoned, sawn asunder, tempted and slain. Some were wanderers in deserts, destitute, afflicted and tormented. But they all had great faith! Faith did not keep them from these things. Faith brought them through these things! And they all came through with a good report! The purpose of Faith is to bring you through every thing that Satan throws at you! No matter what you are going through, hold on to your faith! Do not let anyone tell you that you are going through anything because you do not have enough faith. You do have faith! God has given you faith! It takes far more faith to go through battles than to never have a battle! The greatest people of faith, fight the greatest battles and win the greatest victories!

If you need medication, take it, but do it in faith! If you need a doctor, see one, but see him in faith! If you need therapy, get it, but do it in faith! If you need prayer, get it, but pray in faith!

Whatever you do, do it in faith! Wherever you are, whatever you are going through, in your spirit, rise up in faith and stand on God's Word! You will come through and you will come through with a good report! Your faith is designed to do just that for you!

As I said in the beginning of this book, I have preached and taught faith all of my ministerial life. I have seen thousands of miracles of every kind, on myself, my family and on thousands of people to whom I have ministered.

Because of my teaching, some people think that I have never been sick or that I live some kind of weird, supernatural life. That is not true. I am battered by Satan, just like anyone else. Therefore, I do everything I can to block Satan's attacks.

Do I carry life and health insurance? Yes!

Do I take medicine? Yes!

Do I see a doctor regularly? Yes!

Do I take Flu shots? Yes!

Do I exercise regularly? Yes, I walk daily.

Do I try to eat right? Yes, (most of the time)!

Do I believe God? Absolutely!

You see, I can have greater faith because I know that I have done all that I can do to keep myself healthy. Satan cannot accuse me and tell me that he has a right to afflict me because I have not done what I was supposed to do! I can rebuke him, because I know that I have done my part and God has done His part, at Calvary. Thus I can stand on faith, with full assurance that I will come through with a good report! Faith will bring me through every storm! That is what it is designed to do! That is the purpose of faith!

CHAPTER 8

THE RESULTS OF FAITH

In forty years of preaching faith, I have seen nearly every kind of miracle that one can imagine! I have seen the lame walk, the blind see, the dumb talk, cancer healed and even the dead raised! Thousands of miracles have taken place! A full set of books could not hold all of them! So I just want to share a few stories here. I want to increase your faith and encourage you to believe for your miracle!

FROM THE MENTAL HOSPITAL

Mary Ann was in a mental hospital. She had been on drugs. She had taken a drug that actually blew her mind. The therapists had told her husband that she would never come out of the hospital. They even told him that by the laws of the state, he could divorce her, because she was declared insane. This shook her husband so much that he turned to Christ! He sought help in several places. One night he came to me and asked if I would talk to his wife. I did not know him or his wife, but I said I would talk to her. Then someone came up and told me that she was in the Mental hospital and the therapists had given her up. I found out that he could get her out on pass, so I agreed to talk to her. For several weeks, I got nowhere with her. She had multiple personalities. Sometimes I was talking to one personality and sometimes to another.

One day, out of desperation, I told her that I loved her and wanted to help her. She replied, "You don't love me. God doesn't love me. Nobody loves me." I told her again that I loved her, then she said something that changed my life! She said, "If you knew me you would not love me." I thought of how often people walk around saying they love one another. Even in churches we say those words. But when we get to know the faults and failures of others, we begin to shun and avoid them. Our love grows cold.

I silently prayed and asked God to tell me what to say. God gave me a Word of Wisdom arid I said, "There is *nothing you can* tell me about yourself that would stop me from loving you." I have thought about this many times since. What a powerful statement this is! Even husbands and wives cannot say this to one another. We all tend to love people as long as they do like we want them to do. Unconditional love is scarce in this world. When I made this statement to Mary *Ann,* she angrily spat out every rotten thing that she had ever done. She told me how bad she had been and how sinful she had lived. For forty five minutes she went on. When she finished, she said "1 am going to die and go to hell forever." Again God helped me and I said, "Mary Ann, I still love you." Then for the first time, I saw a tear run down her cheek. I knew then that I had the victory! I laid hands on her and rebuked Satan. She was delivered and started a process of renewing her mind. That has been over twenty four years ago! Today, she is my secretary! She is involved in Ministry and has helped numerous people get delivered from drug and alcohol addiction!

FROM THE DEAD

I was in a revival in Lexington N.C. A woman came to service with a baby. The baby boy had been born with a hole in his heart. He had never been able to cry. He could not take his milk. The doctors had told the mother that he would not live and had allowed her to bring him home.

She sat on the front row of the church and while I preached, the baby died! She ran to the altar crying "My baby is dead." The baby had turned blue and a white foam came out of his mouth. There were two nurses in the church and they immediately ran to the altar, with the mother. They felt the Baby's pulse and temple. They looked at me and said, "Brother Hunt, he is dead." I stood there stunned, not knowing what to do. It looked like I should be consoling the mother or making arrangements for the dead baby or something. But I was in the middle of a sermon on faith! Before I knew it, I jumped over the altar, laid my hand on the baby and began to scream, "God raise him from the dead!" I continued screaming for about five minutes. Then, suddenly, the baby took a deep breath! He turned pink and began to cry! Of course, the church went wild!

Six years later, I returned to this same church for revival. A woman walked up to me with a big healthy boy. She said, "Do you remember that baby that died in your service?" I said "Yes, I do." She said, "This is him." I said, "That is the baby that died in my service six years ago?" She said, "Yes and he has never been sick since!"

FROM PERSONAL EXPERIENCE

I have enjoyed wonderful health, since the Lord saved me. I was born with two serious conditions and I had poor health, until I was fifteen years old. At that age, I was given six months to live. I went to a tent meeting and was saved and healed! From that time forward, I never even had a minor surgery or bone break! Then three years ago, on a Saturday morning, The Holy Spirit spoke to me and told me to go to the doctor and be checked out. Many times in my Ministry, the Spirit has shown me other people's conditions and I have been able to minister healing to them. But this time, the Gift was working for me! I had no pain, no symptoms, no discomfort. But I knew that the Spirit was telling me to go to the doctor.

Because it was a Saturday, my wife took me to Urgent care. They did an EKG, a chest x-ray and a blood enzyme test. The doctor, said, "All tests are normal. I cannot find anything wrong with you. I can give you some comfort medicine or I can send you to the hospital for further tests." I asked to be sent to the hospital, because I knew what the Spirit had told me.

At the hospital, they did the same tests and said they could find nothing, but offered to give me a stress test. I told the two cardiologists to do it. So they x-rayed me, put the nuclear medicine in me, put me on the tread mill, then x-rayed me again. They both said, "We are ninety-nine per cent sure that there is nothing wrong with you, but we will give you a catherization, if you want it." Again I told them to proceed.

After the catherization, they both said, "Your veins are pristine. Your heart muscle is strong. If you would like to have a surgeon look at your heart pictures, we will do so." They were finding nothing wrong with me and yet I knew that the Spirit had told me to come. So I had a surgeon look at the pictures of my heart. He saw something that they had missed! He saw that my heart was fine, but my aorta was enlarged! He explained it to me like this: "When someone has a heart attack, they usually recover, if it is caught in time. But when someone suddenly dies and has had no previous symptoms, it is usually from a ruptured aorta. Only one in ten survive this. Your aorta is enlarged and it will rupture, within the next five years." I asked what could be done about it and he told me that he could take out a part of my aorta and replace it with a plastic tube. I said "Do it!" Then he began to explain: "When we do a bypass surgery, we hook you to a machine, to keep your blood flowing. But when we do an aorta replacement, there will be a time when your blood is not flowing, so we freeze your brain, to prevent brain damage. You could have a stroke, you could have brain damage or you could die."

I came through the surgery fine. Then the next night, I started bleeding, internally. At some point, they said I died. Yet I remember everything that went on in that room! Physically, I was laying there on the bed with my eyes closed and unconscious. Yet my spirit came out of my body and I saw and heard everything that went on! The Doctor drilled a hole in my side and inserted a chest tube, hooked to a pump, to pump out the blood I was losing. My blood pressure dropped to forty over thirty-five. They gave me six units of blood. They called the STAT team. I saw the two nurses run down the hall and into my room. They took my covers and gown off. They bathed me with a conducive liquid. They tied my hands and feet to the bed. They had to zap my left leg, because my chest was cut open. They zapped me twice. It felt just like liquid lightening going through me. At that point, I got back into my body! My heart has beat over one hundred million times since then!

HAVE FAITH!

I share these stories with you, to encourage you! Never give up! Never give in to fear! Faith is not fear! Fear hinders faith! There are people who allow fear to rule their lives! Even Christians who love God dearly, will tolerate fear in their thinking! Some will excuse their fear, in the name of precaution. They will say they are just taking caution, But there is a difference in caution and fear. As I have already said, it is right to do all you can for yourself. But it must be done in faith! You must cast out all fear.

The Bible says that those who have a fear of death are in bondage all their lives. You must have faith like Ester: "If I perish, I perish." (Est. 4:15) You must have faith like Paul: "I am not only ready to be bound, but I am ready to die for Christ." (Acts 21:13) "For me to live is Christ, but to die is gain." (Phil. 1:21) You must have faith like David: "Yea though I walk through the valley of the shadow of death, I will fear no evil." (Ps. 23)

Know this: Nothing that has happened in your life is a surprise to God! He knew what was coming your way before it got there. He has already planned the outcome, before you got in the circumstances! Your footsteps are all ordered! Now look up in Faith and praise Him! Lift up your head and the King of Glory will come in! He will always cause you to triumph! You are more than a conqueror in Christ! You are the apple of His eye! You are the righteousness of God, in Christ! His good thoughts toward you are more than the grains of sand by the sea shore! No weapon formed against you shall prosper! Every tongue that shall judge you, will be condemned! Greater is He that is in you than he that is in the world!

If you can believe, all things are possible to him that believes! (Mk. 9:23)

9 781602 667457